PolitiCool Right

by Joe Ricken

POLITI*COOL* RIGHT

A Beginner's Guide to Conservatism

by

JOE RICKEN

LUMINARE PRESS
EUGENE OREGON

PolitiCool Right is available for puchase online or at:

www.politicoolright.com

Follow the PolitiCool Right blog into politics and life's expeditions at:

josephricken.wordpress.com

Contents

Chapter 1
What's This Book All About?

This book is entitled *PolitiCool Right*, and in the pages that follow I will make the case for political conservatism using logic as my foundation. The goal will be to show you, the readers, why logic and conservatism make better sense, or are "cooler," than liberalism. I use the word *cool* as a superlative in an effort to make the book seem less like the usual stuffy political books. Thus, knowing what this book is not might prepare you for what you are poised to read further. Most books about politics, or at least those I've skimmed, can be somewhat pretentious, self-righteous, loquacious and, frankly, filled with far too much statistical information. My attempt will be to limit the previously mentioned attributes; all of which would otherwise probably bore the casual reader. I also won't fill this book with endless satire in an effort to entertain because, let's face it, funny is in the delivery. What you can expect, however, is an easy going approach to explaining why it is that I believe conservatism is cooler than liberalism.

As mentioned, this book will not follow the usual blueprint of most political books for these reasons: first, I don't believe I have a higher moral existence than most people so I won't pretend as though my conservatism is divinely inspired. I do have opinions about spirituality but they don't drive my politics. Second, I'll try not to sound smarter than I really am. Third, and maybe the most important, I will not fill this book with constant figures and charts and statistics in an effort to prove that conservatism is superior by way of mathematics. Many political books have immense amounts of "information" in the way of percentages and historical data and such. This book will not. In fact, I will not have done countless hours of research in writing this manuscript.

The attempt will be to convince or perhaps strengthen the reader's positions from what knowledge resides and bounces around in my head. The reason for the statistical, data and overall numbers omission is simple and twofold. The first reason is that, to be honest, it can be pretty boring. Even for an "armchair" politician, such as I consider myself to be, too much data and reference to past political strategies and/or voting patterns is just plain boring. My conservative viewpoints are not based on numbers but rather on logic. Constantly having to cite data would certainly not keep me motivated to write, thus I'd imagine the everyday reader would become bored as well.

The bigger truth behind the numbers omission is

this: not only do I not want to cite and write about politics numerically, but I don't have the time to do hours and hours of research. I don't have the kind of spare time it would take to do research that, frankly, I don't think would bolster my point. What this book will contain will be my reasoning based on logic; which resides in my head from years of absorbing politics. For better or for worse, this book will not have been tirelessly researched upon completion. Again, the attempt will be to either convince or strengthen the reader's position by way of my understanding of conservatism based on logic.

Often liberals and liberal politicians argue in favor of what they want by stirring up emotion and not by relying on logic. Arguing against logic, in my opinion, is akin to trying to reason that the Earth doesn't revolve around the sun. Or perhaps it's like arguing against the fact that everything that lives will die. Immortality is folklore and we know that the Earth is not at the center of the universe, but rhetoric can go a long way in convincing people that the obvious is not true. One might think that those are objective examples whereas politics has many more subjective issues. But that may be one of the biggest fables of them all and why perhaps liberals exist in the numbers they do. Politics does have concrete answers and conservatism cements its conclusions in logic.

Now I must admit political books are not for everyone. My hope is for those who think of conservatives as stuffy and uptight, and who may read this book, I can break down the stereotypes by explaining why I believe conservatism is cooler than liberalism. Too often people who don't know much about politics or consider themselves to be liberal, think of conservatives as a bunch of self-righteous do-gooders who never curse and don't drink beer. Or they think conservatives are "red-necks" who drive large trucks, drink too much beer, and hunt more often than they read. Or perhaps liberals just think that their version of political theory is more intellectually evolved. As for me…I don't hunt but I do drink beer. But the truth is that conservative theory is the more intellectual of the ideologies, despite one's beer intake. And once it's fully understood, it just "clicks" for most people; such as it did for me many years ago.

Ultimately this book will give logical explanations of conservatism and the solutions it offers to some of the political and social issues of the day; which will simultaneously reveal the "coolness" of conservatism. This book certainly won't be for everyone, but it could be. There are many people on both sides of the political spectrum whose pretentiousness would have them use this book in lieu of toilet paper before they'd read it. They may agree or disagree with its content, but I'm not Washington D.C. elite, a decorated journalist or even a real writer; and I don't pretend to be. Thus I'm guessing that my tone may too simplistic for such exorbitant verbal taste.

As well, there are many apolitical people and those on the fringe of leftism who may not be perfectly clear as to what differentiates the two ideologies. This book could be for them. These folks probably tend to think the subject of politics is too contentious and, in practice, pretty boring. They usually wouldn't read political books. They don't pay a lot of attention to politics, but they should. Even die-hard, blue collared conservatives may not think they need any reinforcement in their political knowledge and thus pass this book by just as fast. Nobody or everybody may or may not think that this book would be something they'd enjoy, but I'm hoping that by this point I've done due diligence to my literary hook and the reading continues.

My hope is that this book will squeeze a little bit of logical, political juice out of those who view politics very skeptically, those who don't view it at all or those whose views on politics are misshaped due to a skewed starting point of political cognizance. It has never ceased to amaze me how many people do not in fact know what, or can explain what, the major differences are in the two political ideologies of left and right. By writing this book, my intention is to show that conservatism does make the most sense, once it's understood. The method behind my strategy is an effort to make politics more understandable and to show why it doesn't need to be a "smart persons" game. Politics is theory first then practice. I know that politics turns a lot of people off because, on the surface, it seems muddled in chaotic and sometimes transparent passion; not to mention legislative procedure less exciting than insurance seminars. But it doesn't have to be boring or abused.

Politics has become a place where people with

small agendas have infiltrated and, consequently, have transformed their petty annoyances into rules and regulations that make our lives more difficult than they need to be. These people use government to push through agendas which require more and more government oversight. The result is a fee, license, permit or fine applicable to every industry or recreation. These regulation creators are elected officials, bureaucrats, or citizen groups but they all want to change something; and most often just for change's sake. But voting and understanding one's vote can put an end to useless government oversight and release this country from the grip of those who want to force a free people into illogical situations. In other words…we can be cool again.

Chapter 2
What Is Conservatism?

I've mentioned already that conservatism is synonymous with logic, but one might ask how do we know what logical is? Surely everybody has got a different definition of logic and who is to say one person's logic isn't another person's padded cell? In politics, logic means deciding an issue or solving a problem with the most sensible conclusion in reference to the original intent of our government. That generally means that those involved in the process take a very objective approach and have an understanding of the concept of limited government; as was envisioned by the creators of our earliest governmental documents. As such, conservatives generally migrate to the Republican Party as the antithesis to this concept is very much on display in the theoretical confines of the Democratic Party.

Political conservative thought is based in logic. In its purest form it takes most of the emotion out of a political decision and draws conclusions outside of those emotions. Conservatives don't shun emotion, they simply understand that emotion is what makes us uniquely human and our level of intelligence gives us the ability to recognize those emotions and rationalize outside of them. Liberalism does not separate emotion from politics. In talking about emotion and the role it plays in liberal governance, it's important to make the distinction between it and the type of emotion which is more analogous with love and respect. The emotion which tends to guide liberal policy is akin to overreaction, guilt and hysteria. The kind of emotion that is easy to stir up but just as easy to see through because it generally has no substance to it. It's like…trouble making.

Conservatism, however, is not simply making decisions quickly and based on primal instinct, either. Some may argue that making a decision void of emotion, is like a dog making the decision to sniff something or urinate on a tree, which is instinctual for a dog. However, the fact is that instinct and emotional overreaction are closer characteristically speaking to each other than they are to logic and reason. If one makes a decision too rapidly, without much thought, that can be as foolish as basing a decision on too much emotion.

A good example of this kind of emotion, in a simplified presentation, would be an instance in which someone is told something second-hand which offends them; subsequently getting upset at the supposed guilty party. In other words, someone gets upset over some gossip. If their first thought is to call up the offending gossiper and give them a piece of their mind, that's acting emotional; because as is the case most often, gossip tends to be exaggerated. A few days later the truth may come out that the rumors weren't so true. It's then that the angry person realizes that they should have recognized the situation for what it was and dealt with it reasonably instead of being instinctually emotional. Often liberal politics wants to react emotionally without regard for what the potential results might be.

Before I proceed, allow me to make a point to clarify the conservative stance as it pertains to liberals or people who vote Democrat and the theory behind the ideology of liberalism. Conservatives don't take issue, per se, with everyday persons on the left. We generally understand that liberals exist in the numbers they do because there are politicians who desire power, and they get it, and votes, by playing to other people's emotions. The politicians themselves use false emotion to attract and extract real emotion out of people who may have a tendency toward political feelings of guilt and overreaction. They understand that their rhetoric makes these people want to be compassionate and it tugs at their emotional uncertainty, thus getting them votes.

Conservatism simply means applying logic and reason in governing and making every effort to leave emotion out in an attempt to govern objectively. In essence, conservatism does not use emotion to lead people to believe that government is their best answer to a problem. Conservatism does not give people something they're led to believe they need but do not. The ideology is rooted in self-reliance over dependence. Emotional people, however, will tend to gravitate toward messages which shift responsibility away from the individual. Politicians and other liberal mouthpieces will then levy the perceived injustices at large, usually wealthy, entities. It's easy for liberal politicians to create villains to get votes because they have a large pulpit and the impression of legislative watchdog by virtue of being voted into office.

Let me take time to illustrate the way emotion can take precedence over logic and force some people into making irrational decisions by way of another simply presented or, "real world," example. In the game of golf the object is to finish each hole, and subsequently the round of 18 holes, with the lowest possible score. Each swing of the club is tallied as a stroke and the player who uses the least amount of strokes to get the ball to the hole will win. Each hole is different in length and geography and thus requires a focused approach for every individual hole. One cannot simply hit it as hard as they will every time because of the terrain and proximity to the hole. In other words, the golfer must think his or her way to the hole. Again, this is an example of emotion, not a commentary on liberal golfers.

In our example I'll use two golfers named Larry and Cramer (Liberal and Conservative) playing a hole together. It's a par 5 which means the average golfer should be able to get the ball in the hole in about 5 shots. Getting the ball onto the putting green in three shots is also what's considered average, or regulation. Players can and sometimes do get to the putting green in two shots on a par 5, but it's rare. It takes a great shot and some luck, thus most golfers will attempt to get to the green with their third shot. But some golfers will try anything to get an edge…

In our example, Larry and Cramer are both playing their respective *second* shots on a par 5 hole from about the same place on the fairway. Larry, wanting to gain an emotional edge over his opponent, tries to get to the green on his second shot. He doesn't, however, and instead swings too hard and almost misses the ball entirely. He curses the ball and gets visibly upset. Cramer, however, hits it softer and sets himself up to get to the green on the next shot. In golf, that's called "laying up." Larry most likely justified his attempt with emotion. He knew if he made the green on his second shot it would give him an emotional and literal edge over his opponent. But what he failed to consider was that if he missed, there may be trouble. Now he will yield a few strokes to his opponent as he tracks down his ball.

In this scenario, it makes more sense to "lay up" like Cramer did than to smash away at it like Larry. But Larry was overwhelmed with the potential glory of a great shot. He's no doubt heard heroic stories told daily around the bar at happy hour of amazing golf shots made. Larry would want the emotional high that accompanies an incredible shot. Cramer, however, better understood that the safety of "laying up" should outweigh the risk of a bad miss. In golf, as in politics, you don't get a do-over after a bad miss.

This example is not meant to imply that all conservatives "lay up" and that all liberals are inherent risk takers. But often liberalism justifies its conclusions on what feels good at the moment, and not necessarily on what is best for the long term. Therein lies one of the greatest differences in the two philosophies when it come the process of governing. Conservative thought, though perhaps not edgy, doesn't assume risk for risk's sake. It leaves out the emotion of landing it on the green in two shots because the potential for a negative outcome is reduced by playing it smarter. Not to mention if one misses badly and gets upset, they look very uncool.

And...

Most people probably consider themselves to be logical people when it comes to their everyday decisions in life; nobody wants to consider themselves to be illogical. However, when emotion gets injected into politics, it's harder for people to see the contrasts. Conservatives generally see political issues as a black and white whereas liberal politicians tend to make the issues grayer, if you will. The grayness of their rhetoric makes it more difficult to notice the stark contrasts, which better illuminate the logical conclusions. Gray is not always a bad thing as it can make for some great literature; it's just not the best idea when applied to governing.

Liberal politicians aren't usually concerned with long term and real sustainability. They often use the vastness of the government, both federally and locally, to swallow up their solutions when they don't make fiscal sense. Their logic is to play big and maybe gamble a little because the merits are in the intentions of the bad shot and shouldn't be judged on the scorecard. Thus the public is often handed solutions that look to spend tax payer money to alleviate a problem which is manufactured through creative hyperbole. They are more concerned with how to get that emotional edge than they are with making sure the solution will actually make sense in the real world.

We see examples of this all over liberal policies as it pertains to social welfare and other social programs. Often the first thought from liberal politicians is to simply spend some money band-aiding the problem. Many social programs don't go far enough to encourage the people they serve to strategize and eventually work their way off of the program. Most programs simply hand out goods or services, which keeps the recipients situation static if not worsening. The desire to support oneself is inherent but if receiving aid is free or cheap, the ease of obtaining aid may supersede the appetite for self-preservation. However, liberal politicians will tout their efforts as noble despite the outcome. Even if the programs are proving to be undermined and sloppily financed, the appearance of "doing something" will be what matters to the emotional person.

If we extend the example of Larry and Cramer to the internals of a Las Vegas casino, we might ask: who would be best suited to gamble money that isn't theirs? (Such as the government does with tax revenue) If a friend of Larry and Cramer wanted to give one of the men $500 to gamble for him, in the absence of gambling knowledge, who might we assume he'd choose? The answer for most people would be Cramer. Even if the third party were to make a deal that the gambler keep a percentage of the winnings, we might still assume that Cramer would be the choice, despite Larry's penchant for taking risks; which in gambling can pay off quicker on bets with lesser odds. Cramer, however, would most likely gamble the way he approaches the golf shot, trying to maximize his potential with smart play.

The purpose of these analogies is to illustrate the different sides of the political spectrum and how politicians might react in situations that can have an effect on the public. If one is prone to emotion or desires power in politics, then they may take a more risky approach to governing; which includes spending citizen tax revenue. In analyzing the decisions made by politicians on the left, one would have to conclude that they aren't concerned with results as much as intent. The money they're gambling with isn't theirs. For that matter, any politician who has a disregard for how their decisions will impact their constituents, either as collective debt incurred or on the basis of fairness, is reckless in their approach to governing. The fact is that governing with objectivity is not a difficult concept to embrace or understand.

The responsibilities of the collective purse, which the citizens ultimately give to politicians, coupled with legislative authority gives elected officials a great amount of power. True conservative politicians do not revel in such power but rather they understand the duties and obligations that come with holding office. They want to spend tax collected money wisely and with thrift and they do not believe in transferring wealth by means of excessive social programs. They genuinely believe in the capabilities and opportunities of every citizen and desire to create an environment, via government, that fosters fairness. The easiest way to do that is to limit the government's role as a part of society.

As I mentioned previously, I'm not a political insider and I have never had aspirations to run for office. For whatever reason, I took an interest in politics very early on and I have spent over 20 years studying politics and paying attention in general. As a qualifier, I hold a bachelor's degree in political science and a master's degree in education in the field of social studies. I mention this because most persons do not know what the real difference is, politically, between liberals and conservatives (Democrats and Republicans respectively), and I want to share my knowledge. As well, this book is subtitled as a "beginner's guide," thus I want to make it easy to understand.

If we can conclude that logic is how conservatives in politics tend to make decisions and emotion guides many liberal policies, then what can we say about how this translates to the methods of governing? Politicians can be put into parties and those parties have one major line drawn between them. Thinking back to our golf analogy, conservatives would tend to "lay up" on the political golf course using a measured approach while liberals may shoot for sweeping change guided by emotion and implement it haphazardly. Conservatives have a strategy to play for par and not become terribly risky with the people's government.

Consequently, the disparities are very salient but often misunderstood. The indisputable difference between conservatives and liberals is this: Less Government vs. More Government. It's truly that simple and no apolitical or otherwise politically unsure person ought to be convinced otherwise. Conservative politicians begin with the notion that their role as an elected official is to govern objectively but to continue to adhere to the principle of limited government. This is not because a conservative politician or official does not want to work, but rather it's due to the belief, rooted in origin, that the less the government is involved in the lives of Americans, the better off Americans are.

The belief in a limited government, which was envisioned by the founders, is accompanied by the trust that Americans will take personal responsibility seriously and not look to the government for answers to all of their questions. In fact, conservatives will espouse personal responsibility as a cornerstone of what makes America so grand. The country is not led by a dictator, thus Americans shouldn't look to the government for answers which they are perfectly capable of resolving without government intervention. When too much authority is granted and not kept in check, the result is often petty agendas being enacted into illogical laws.

The subsequent question must be asked as well: what is the political draw for emotion based people to a larger role for the government? The answer, in my opinion, is that liberals have a learned perception that victimization is more prevalent than it truly is. Their neighborhoods, the country and the world are full of disparity and rather than understand that this discrepancy is derived from equal opportunity, they will feel as though there must be some larger force at work which creates this human imbalance. Simply waking up in the morning does not bestow upon someone the necessities or the creature comforts of modern day human life. Yet liberals will attempt to utilize governing forces as a means to ultimately equalize the outcomes of citizens.

The overarching feeling which begins liberalism is one of guilt, which is followed by blame and ultimately vindicated by divisive rhetoric on the part of liberal politicians. Eventually, liberal citizens come to believe that this disparity must be fixed and can only be done by the government. The dirty secret is that the liberal politicians know that it can't be fixed by government; because nothing is wrong with differing lifestyles. What attempting to fix it does is create a dependency on government to justify the feelings of guilt, which in turn leads to willingness on the part of citizens to go along with government despite their own best interests. It tends to make people think that more, not less, government is what makes life better.

Conservatism, however, is not the first step toward anarchy. Government, in the eyes of conservatives, is a necessary entity and one that can, with the right people in charge, be good and moral. With the right attitude and the right people working for it, the government can and should be a part of American life. If, however, it is perceived as a tool to push personal agendas that are not logical, then that's when it becomes frighteningly influential and can become big enough to negatively impact the lives of people.

Conversely, conservatives are not conspiracy ridden to the extent that a "big brother" scenario is a constant war drum that gets beat. But when one considers that the liberal ideology is rooted in a trust in government, the result can only be a constantly growing bureaucratic body. Conservatives will agree that technology and human advancement will require the need for some new and continued governmental oversight, however when a bloated bureaucracy begins to grow exponentially people will get sloppy and the burdens shift to the citizenry. The task then becomes one of trying to dissolve reckless spending and taper the growth of unnecessary government.

If politicians use logic when deciding the new rules or regulations, it will foster an environment that does not create bureaucracy without focused purpose. Too often liberal politicians have 'knee-jerk' reactions to issues, thus implementing regulations and rules based on emotion and not pragmatism. Every little emotional issue has the potential to beget more little regulations. Remember, the liberal citizens have a trust in government while the liberal politicians take advantage of that. Emotional people will tend to favor more bureaucracy because of their inherent mistrust with particular people. They are generally more willing to sacrifice small freedoms in the name of protection, whereas conservatives will favor the luxury to be free of bureaucrats dictating to them how they should live. One can think of many small regulations on things such as: cigarettes, salt, bicycle helmets, seat belts, trans fats and carbon dioxide to name a few. All of which have regulations in an effort to protect people from themselves.

Elected officials, under the guise of safety, will implement small rules to satisfy their sense of duty when the status quo is usually acceptable based upon a free market. As an example, many liberal politicians in states and cities across the nation have banned smoking in private institutes. Going so far as to require smoking away from doorways and even banning it outdoors in some state run areas. Whether one smokes or not, having to stand 25 feet from a doorway of an establishment to smoke is paranoia plain and simple. The citizens need to be reminded that they are governed in-so-much as they are the consenting ones. In other words, the citizens tell the bureaucrats how they want to be governed and not the other way around. But they still can't use government to tell private companies how to operate their business.

Of course, regulations and government oversight is not completely unnecessary. I've stated already that with the right attitude, government has a purpose and can coexist with private enterprise just fine. There are logical places to implement regulatory measures to ensure the well-being of citizens. For example, the water supply of a city should be regulated and maintained but not so much that it is also at the mercy of hysterical engineers. Other silly regulations abound such as calorie calculator mandates on restaurant menus. We must ask is it the government's role to regulate the caloric intake of restaurant goers by mandating that caloric calculators be provided on the menus of private businesses? This and other rather silly regulations are precise examples of what conservatives refer to when they talk about governing just to govern.

Power in the hands of the wrong people will be abused, slowly and without much notice. It may not be conspiratorial, but it will eventually lead to larger and larger government roles in society. Again, that's what makes liberal people comfortable. They may not be colluding to eventually implement full blown communism, but they fail to understand the real repercussions of allowing a government to grow beyond what is logical and reasonable. As mentioned earlier, liberals often see victimization where there isn't any and thus they believe that the government is a body without bias; which is why its growth gets mostly overlooked. But that's a more dangerous notion because there is very little oversight on the overseers.

Conservatives do not want to hand over any freedoms unjustly to the government because some elected officials or bureaucrats think they know better than the people. Citizens are very capable of solving communal problems without politicians playing to the emotions of a few. Over-governing leads to government personnel believing they have an almost messianic appeal, due mostly to the willfulness of constituents playing along. But politicians are just people and not lords. In most cases, the "regulators" of industry and politicians themselves have very little private sector experience with which to draw from. That means they will set the rules while monitoring through a very narrow lens. And that is simply not cool.

Chapter 3
What's The Problem With Walmart?

Liberal folks usually get their cues from liberal politicians spouting off about the dangers and downside to "Corporate America." They believe that somehow large companies, such as Walmart, have unyielding power that forces customers to shop and buy from their discounted shelves. Walmart tends to be a favorite target of the left. Liberals will often make reference to what they see as negative effects that corporations have on America. The rumbling diatribes are usually full of platitudes about wages and greed. Myself, I think it's due to a pretentiousness that many on the left have and not as much about the talking points. But that's what they hear from politicians and left-leaning commentators who prostitute their opinion about money from high atop their own financial hill. Emotional people, however, will get an emotional high from blaming someone else for the fact that they are not owners of everything they want.

Even more criticism is leveled toward Corporate

America from liberals who feel that larger companies have too much influence in politics. Money certainly does make its way into politics but logic would tell us that the problem is neither the money nor the donor. If money ends up having an influence with a particular politician or bureaucrat, it is common sense to cast the blame where it's due: the receiver. When a transaction between corporate donor and politician is made and the understanding is a quid-pro-quo, the offense must lie with the politician. If we think about it rationally, where's the problem, the offer or the acceptance?

The answer to that will go a long way toward understanding why it is that conservatives often view government as the entity with the most negative influence in the country. There's an old saying about where the "buck" stops; in politics it stops with the politician. Elected officials play by a thinly monitored set of rules and they are well aware of that fact. The result of an election can give a politician years of virtually untouchable power. Within that time frame they can be instrumental in enacting legislation that makes no logical sense and approve reckless spending which affects the common person for years. That should be far scarier than Walmart and Corporate America in general, who can't force the citizen to do anything they do not choose to do. No private enterprise has that kind of power; they can merely offer competitive pricing. If every shopper decided not to shop at Walmart, then Walmart would be history.

When we understand the victim mentality of the

left it makes sense that they would fear and chastise large corporations. People who operate and run large companies are generally well compensated and therein again lies the problem with liberals. They naturally want to find victims and they'll usually look down the corporate ladder first; griping that workers are not treated fairly. Next they will make the argument that large companies kill off smaller, local businesses. But what they fail to realize is that in a market economy, every consumer has choices. They have the choice to shop where they want, to work where they do, and choose with whom they do business.

It's a dangerous precedent to set for the government to be led to action by emotion when it comes to dealing with Corporate America. The market usually takes pretty good care of itself because people invest themselves into what they do. But a strong economy and a healthy society cannot allow the government to tell corporations how they should pay their employees or when to stop growing. The market will police that kind of behavior by way of profit margins. However, the United States government tries all too often to over-police the market and it ends up with a greater negative effect. For example, if anti-trust laws are enforced too narrowly as to how big a company can get, that puts immense power in the hands of those that get to decide how big is too big. Subsequently that kind of government intrusion kills job creation.

As well, we should not forget that business is cyclical because technology is constantly changing and people don't like the same things forever. An example is movie rentals. It began with small video stores and then it became a few large retail chains that had all the business. Now it's kiosk rental or streaming online. The point is that the market will change and people will be the driving force behind that change; it shouldn't be government trying to keep the status quo alive. The government has tremendous power and that should really scare the hell out of the average person. But the good news is we have the power of our vote to put people into office that won't use their position to invoke fear.

One should think about the vast power the government has before casting their next vote. The question should be asked: "do I want that power to grow?" Government, by way of legislation and regulation can and does force citizens into adhering to rules that make little sense. Bureaucracy is created with the intention of being efficient but soon the power structure of government positions become overbearing. Government agencies do not work in conjunction well with one another and often it is up to the citizen to interpret what is necessary to get through a labyrinth of regulatory red tape. Defenders may excuse the inefficiency, again, by pointing out the intention of the regulation but they fail to realize that good intentions should still be accountable and managed appropriately.

The same power is highly visible in terms of taxation. When money is taxed from one person and then given to another, the appearance is one of charity. But is it really charitable to take and then give? The true charity is coming from those being taxed at a rate which makes their lives difficult...in an effort to support people who will not do for themselves. When politicians have the ability to tax and spend there is no doubt going to be an end game in mind; which for them is reelection.

The people should remember that government really doesn't have any money. It assumes responsibility for the printing of money but the only money they have to spend comes from the citizens making money in a free market. Every government function, from paving roads to food stamps is paid for by hard working citizens. And to a sane person, redistribution of their hard earned money is loathsome. That's not to say, however, that government shouldn't tax. But logic and objectivity would bring with it the understanding that the money being spent is not "free" money but rather money that was hard earned by someone else. Without such understanding the privilege of spending citizen's money gets abused. People can shop anywhere, but they cannot hide from a power hungry government. We ought to fear the authority to take someone's money more than cheap toothpaste on sale at Walmart.

Accountability Is Scarce

Let's digress just a bit so it's understood that conservatives do believe in a strong, functioning government. There are specific and necessary duties government must carry out because the private sector is not the most logical place with which to create particular community attributes. That is to say that there are services that societies need that the private sector simply should not carry out. Not because it can't but rather it makes logical sense to have the government use collective funds to implement them. Some examples include: the roadway system, police and fire, military and the printing of money. Outside of some of the necessities, the rest of what government spends money on is subjective and could be scaled back immensely.

Many of the agenda driven expenditures of government are frivolous and a majority of the services could be handled by the private sector instead. For example, a place like the DMV could be outsourced to the private sector and there would be much more accountability. Right now citizens have no place to turn as the DMV is a chaotic, red-tape driven bureau of the government. If given to the private sector to handle, there would be accountability because it would be consumer based and driven. As it stands, there is no legitimate form of oversight for government agencies. If people are unhappy waiting two hours to renew a driver's license…they're S.O.L. The consumer can hold Walmart accountable with their feet, but they're handcuffed when it comes to holding government service bureaus to account.

The fact that accountability is scarce in government makes it hard for the average citizen to really trust that there is objective governing happening. Some might argue that different branches and facets of government keep each other "in check," and to a degree there are some checks and balances. But it doesn't stop the ridiculous regulations and silly little rules we get handed to us. If a local bureaucratic body or elected team wants to enact agenda laws such as those that outlaw plastic bags at grocery stores in favor of forcing the retailer to charge consumers for paper bags, it's difficult to stop the absurdity.

So it can be said that in fact government does scare rational, logical people because there are few limits to what it can do and even fewer avenues citizens can take to oversee the overseers. That's why conservatives want people in those offices that understand the notion of limitations and do not want the government to grow into any larger a body than that which is functionally necessary. Conservative politicians hold the offices they do because they believe in this principle and genuinely want to ensure that a bloated government is not what gets handed to citizens. The exact opposite is true of most Democratic politicians. They see government as a tool to get things done that don't otherwise need doing. But they enjoy having that power because power is their emotion and their campaign rhetoric is designed to push feelings of guilt in an effort to push their agendas.

The issue with a large and ever expanding government is that it requires an ever expanding purse through the taxation of its citizens. Thus, when fees for licensing go up seemingly every year it causes doubt and mistrust on the part of citizens that government is spending the money wisely. The assumption then grows that people in government are not taking their responsibility seriously enough to understand that the money they get to implement their social agendas is not a magic pot of gold. If there are constant funding gaps between the cost of services and the tax revenue then the government is not budgeting correctly. It's that simple.

There truly is a lot of money spent on maintaining government entities, programs and policies. Once a program or bureaucracy is created, whether there was ever a real need, it is extremely hard to discontinue it if needed. Despite the fact that the money to fund some programs is lacking, there are always people in government pining for their existence. Not to mention that there are whole constituencies that get built on free money and services provided by tax payer money. That is powerful stuff. When citizens receive endless aid and it is defended as charitable, then there is little tax payers can do unless those being taxed excessively begin to vote for people who want limited government.

Conservatives believe in the power of the individual and not the government. When the size and scope of the government is limited to the lowest levels necessary, that's when people can and will be their best. But when there are people desirous of power, preying on the weak-willed with the lure of easy and free services, then the job of electing conservatives becomes that much more important. When politicians spend taxpayer money to create a need or develop a voting constituency…that's not cool.

Government as Referee

Most people have watched a sport that involves some kind of referee or umpire so they're aware of the role of those persons in relation to a sporting event. It is to ensure that the playing field creates equal opportunity for both teams to win. Their presence is justified in an effort to equalize the opportunities for the teams involved in the game such that each side has a chance at victory. What they do not do, however, is attempt to equalize the outcome of the game.

I'll start off with an example here to make the larger point. In baseball, basketball, football and most every organized sport, the umpire or referee makes every attempt to ensure the players follow the agreed-upon rules of the game. Most organized sports require some kind of outside, objective perspective so that the players do not cheat their way to victory. But they also add an element of structure to what could otherwise look like chaos on the field or court. That is the government's role in a nutshell: add some structure to society and enforce the rules when they are violated. They must call a fair game.

If, for instance, the referee of a football game over-reached and allowed one team to have 9 points per touchdown and the other six points, it would not be a "level" playing field. Nor would it be fair if the referee changed the score at the end of the game to make a sound defeat seem less humiliating. For example: Team A wins 55-20 over Team B and the referee changes the score to 40-35 to make it appear to be more of an even outcome; taking away points that were earned by Team A and giving them to Team B. Even if Team A were a more organized bunch and far more motivated for victory than Team B, it still would not be fair. Team A shouldn't be penalized for a lack of preparation on the part of Team B.

Unfortunately, if we look around we see governments at all levels doing exactly this kind of faux refereeing. They attempt to equalize outcomes far too often. There are special rules that apply to some and not to others. There are rules that tax people at different rates based on how their motivation has benefited them financially. The more motivated one is to be successful, the higher rate of tax they pay if they are successful. We have to ask ourselves if that is really a fair and objective role for the government to take? There are plenty of people who are very motivated in life to succeed in particular industries which can bring wealth. And conversely there are others motivated to succeed in historically low paying but very rewarding humanitarian fields. This gets back to the disparity in human behavior that the left has real trouble understanding.

Citizens ought not fret over what someone else has that they do not. More importantly, they should not look to the government, point their fingers, and demand that they get someone else's points. People have the opportunity to be whatever they want to be. Thus, we should all concentrate on how we can make our own homes better and improve our own lives from the inside out. That sounds pretty cool to me.

And just because some people are wealthy, does not mean that someday only a few people will own all of the wealth. If the government referees the game right, Team A needs Team B to compete. It's not a game if Team A is the only team on the field. However, there are many worldly examples of what happens when it's the government that decides it will control all of the wealth. It's called communism and it pretty much stinks.

As a referee, the government can ensure that the playing field is leveled by upholding citizen's rights and granting equal access to those things which government assumes responsibility. Such things like equal protection under the law also certainly level the playing field. It's important for the voter to remember that it's not the government personnel who are special; it's the producers in society. In the example of the ball game, one would argue that the spectators attend to watch the way the game is played by the players, not how it's refereed. But too often government acts as an over-officiating referee and inserts itself into the lives of everyday citizens who do not need to be called out for a foul. Politicians and bureaucrats cannot seem to refrain from the temptation of inserting their policy ideas and agendas into the economy or society.

The ideal for government is to be mostly static and to not take a proactive approach to implementing new regulations and laws on society. As a referee they should only blow the whistle when appropriate and not try to dictate the outcome of the game. They need to resolve issues with logic and avoid the appeal of over-refereeing what they see in their communities. They shouldn't over-govern, over-spend, or over-legislate; rather they should mostly oversee and maintain. The community in general doesn't need the government to solve every issue for it. It's better if the citizenry can work it out on their own, the way a free people will.

Rounding It Out

We've used a couple examples of how liberalism can be more emotion-based as it pertains to governing and how that emotion generally attracts liberal folks to the idea of a larger government. As well, I've given my opinion as to how liberal politicians tend to use government to attract constituents with the end game being to push small agendas through to law.

These observations are not meant to be an exercise in malice or bitterness but rather a conclusion from a conservative point-of-view which considers most political issues to be simple and absolute in resolution. That's because a logical and objective conclusion rarely needs redefinition despite being challenged by hyperbolic opinions. If, however, a person is influenced at their starting point of political cognizance by persons guided by emotion then they will naturally gravitate to the political message which most aggressively displays agitation. As a result, they will look for ways to ensure that others fit into their envisioned way of life.

A point to keep in mind during this endeavor into politics is that conservatives arrive at their conclusions because there is tremendous confidence in the Constitution of the United States. It's especially important to note that the idea of limited government is not something that conservatives simply made up. It is the recurring theme of most documentation we have from the period of time which was the inception of the republic. As humans, our rights are not granted to us by the government, they are protected by the government. The founders of America, though trapped in a world which devalued some people's existence, understood that in order for the country to continue to evolve and thrive it would have to be free from the overreach of a powerful central government. Ironically, it was probably on account of that understanding that the country has evolved socially to the point it has.

The fight to limit government has only gotten more difficult because liberal politicians have figured out that they can use the government in ways that suit their interests. For that matter, any politician can use the government in duplicitous ways, but liberals will do it while wearing a philanthropic veil. In other words, they'll use their power in office to push for illogical conclusions while claiming they're being humanitarian. They often become referees who want to control the game because they tend to view their role in government as "protector."

They will create villains and sound the alarm of class warfare and victimization in an effort to keep their position of power. The transparency of the filthy rich, liberal politician crying foul over income disparity should be proof enough that they do not really care about resolving such matters. For if they did, they would work to encourage folks to follow their lead in pursuit of financial bliss; but they don't because they seem to like being the keepers of the means and the end.

In seeing their role as a protector of sorts, liberal politicians can convince people that they sometimes need protecting even from themselves. We see examples of this when governing persons enact restrictions on things they deem not good for the public. Unfortunately, they end up convincing a large number of constituents that things like trans-fats in foods are a danger that needs the almighty government to shield them from. Or perhaps they use their position in government to convince people that the rich among them are somehow taking advantage of people. They then use that emotion to raise taxes on the few to appease the many. But a government should not work that way. That's not cool. All persons and industries should be represented fairly regardless of how easily social disdain can be levied on them; because powerful people can turn regular people into villains if it suits them.

Chapter 4
What Is Individualism?

A cornerstone of conservatism is the belief in the individual. That varies from liberalism which generally subscribes to the notion of "community over individual." Translated, that means there is a core belief from liberals that the individual needs to work within a community of people in an effort to evolve or transform the whole. The whole, they might say, is greater than the individual. But conservatism believes that individuals working hard to better their lives will inevitably affect the communities they live in. Because when people strive to be great individuals, whatever their definition of great may be, they take pride in their accomplishments and usually continue to advance themselves. That, in turn, creates an expectation that others at least make attempts at bettering themselves.

Individualism draws a lot of its strength from citizens understanding what being responsible for themselves and their actions requires. As a person within a society, one not only needs to depend on themselves, individually, to be successful, but they have to understand that their actions can go a long way in defining the environment around them. That ultimately means not depending on the government for handouts, but also not looking to the government to excuse irresponsible behavior by making it legal; such as abortion laws and drug laws do. Adults need to understand that despite their wisdom of age there are many logical reasons to restrict the government's powers, lest the next generation uses it to really muddy the waters.

Depending too much on the government usually creates sloth-like habits that, once formed, are hard to break. Governmental dependency can make people depend too much on the "community" because they will assume that the slack will be picked up by someone else. That's not to say that all liberals take this perspective, but liberal politicians will go to extremes to ensure that some constituents become dependent because it creates a need and thus retrieves votes. And the emotion of their rhetoric draws in the everyday liberal voter to support the cause. The unfortunate outcome is that certain persons will become very lazy in their approach toward bettering themselves individually because doing as little as possible is the requisite for governmental assistance. In America, people can strive to become whatever they want, but asking the people to aid an apathetic lifestyle is beyond objectionable.

Conservatives will argue that it's the strength of

the individual striving to succeed which makes the community a strong one. Success, however defined, brings with it accountability, assurance and pride. It's too easy for one to get lost in a crowd, so to speak. If someone is constantly hoping that they will become successful by way of government aid as a launching pad, then it's easy to see how the blame game gets started. Nobody, with the exception of lottery winners maybe, will become successful by depending upon others to make their own ends meet.

Again, conservatives are not defining success for the individual but rather reiterating that dependence is not a state of existence that anyone should be happy with. Not everyone will be, nor will want the burdens of, massive financial success. For many, success is in the little aspects of life. But gaining any level of success is much more rewarding when one accomplishes it for themselves. Conservatism doesn't require that everyone become wealthy to be successful but rather that everyone know and understand that they have what it takes to become successful in whatever they endeavor into.

Too often people get fooled by liberal politicians into thinking that other citizens, corporations or wealthy entities are keeping them down. Though it's cliché, the only thing keeping one from succeeding is oneself. But if liberal powers facilitate feelings otherwise, it becomes harder to break that cycle of thinking. Unfortunately, it's all too common for government to create a feeling of individual invisibility because it is becoming easier to fall back on the weight of its overreaching ways.

If it's too easy to get government assistance, then people will stop striving to better their situation. That, in turn, leads to less accountability and a relative lowering of standards that people can expect from one another. As one who has received unemployment insurance, I know the ease by which it can be delivered. It's far too easy and comes with very limited oversight. It appears as though the government bureaucrats are desirous of a seamless transaction in lieu of answerability and responsibility on the part of the recipients. It is tearing down the walls of any incentive to returning to a state of self reliance on the part of the aid seekers. This is developing because the concept of government money is being deliberately altered from the fact that it's had by way of earners paying tax. And subsequently it's those earners being "cool" with allowing the government to redistribute their money for entitlement programs.

In Fairness, Kind of...

As a conservative, it's important to understand what liberalism is and how it's conceived so as to be able to combat it. Liberalism is a powerful tool for people in charge, politicians and bureaucrats, because of its apparent glamorously altruistic message. Liberals may truly want "goodwill" to be done, but they want to delegate that duty elsewhere, which is why liberals don't feel discontent with a larger government. Thus, the liberal politicians use divisive and contemptuous speech, masked as sympathetic and compassionate, to give the appearance that they will use government charitably. It makes emotional people feel like there is something wrong in the "system" and mean people are taking advantage of poor persons; which only government can fix. This is why capitalism and industrialism are seen in such a negative way by the average liberal voter.

A liberal might contend that capitalism can be a real danger and if left unchecked, a capitalist society can become too top heavy with few "winners" and a lot of losers. Capitalism is, in its nature, a survival-of-the-fittest scenario among consumers and producers. In essence, one must provide for themselves to stay alive because there's no inherent quality about capitalism that requires others to care about any other individual's well being. The caring comes from our humanness and the real emotion people possess. But the survival routine makes liberal people a bit uneasy. Perhaps it's the intentional, contentious rhetoric by liberal politicians which leads to the perception of meanness or unfairness about capitalism and industry. In other words, the politicians tell their constituents capitalism is too greed ridden and they believe them.

But we ask…can people be taken advantage of in a capitalist, market economy? The answer is yes they can. Actually, there are many scenarios in a free, market based economy in which people are taken advantage of…in an agreeable kind of way. Capitalism is based on profit and profit is money (or something of value) gained from the sale or trade with another person or persons. Along these lines one could make the argument that any profit is taking advantage of someone by selling or trading something for more than it's worth to the seller. The reason is that it's harder to quantify value based upon the happiness of the consumer in the transaction.

For example, if one is willing to part with a product in exchange for money, the amount deemed acceptable is based upon the fact that the buyer's money is now more valuable to the seller than is the product. Thus, one can conclude that small businesses use the same tactics and equations for success that Walmart does. It's just that Walmart has grown to the point that it's an easy target for liberal politicians based upon the volume of business it does. Liberal mouthpieces can stir up emotion very easily by illuminating the profit margins of large companies. For whatever reason, emotional people will buy into the rhetoric that large companies with large profit margins are ripping someone off.

The reality is, however, that in order for capitalism to succeed it requires there be buyers willing to deem a product worthy of the price. It may be undervalued or marginalized by the seller, but if the buyer finds it to be of value to them, and worthy of the price, they will purchase it. There are very few real "rip-offs" in a capitalist society that can be directly traced to the seller. The exception might be a bad deal being made to a person of challenged mental capacity; which is plain mean. But the buyer holds all the power in a market economy. In most cases, in order to be taken advantage of the buyer has to agree to a bad deal;

which means they've failed to do their homework. This may exclude instances in which legal agreements or good-faith agreements are made and then one party is defrauded. In those cases it is sensible to have a referee in the game to help police blatant bad financial behavior.

Allow me to digress momentarily and say that I understand that as human beings we want to ensure that we are living in a free and fair society. For liberals a system which allows for such glaring discrepancies in lifestyle, on the surface, may appear to be somehow unfair. The emotion that comes with applying victimization is too great sometimes to overlook the legitimacy of a system which favors the individual to the extent that capitalism does. Liberals tend to distrust robust capital activity because they've latched on the association of greed and corruption. Having a referee to interject into the game is not feared as much in their eyes, because the rhetorical affiliation of words like greed plants itself into their psyche.

As a conservative, I don't generally think of greed with a negative connotation when I apply it to a free market economy. In fact, I would go so far as to say that "greed" is a superlative in a system of commerce which, in practice, should allow for individuals to succeed based upon the effort they are willing to put forth. As consumers people need to do their homework and be a little greedy because greed is a self-preserver. The alternative is an ever growing governing body which continues to impose preventative, regulatory measures. One could argue that kind of growth opens the door for carelessness and corruption that stems from the government; and that kind of corruption is harder to ignore or avoid.

Many people on the left believe that only the government can be that unbiased, regulatory body that protects them from getting "ripped off." Or to use the cliché, they need the government to make it harder for the snake oil salesman to sell snake oil. Conservatives would generally like to trust themselves and their own instincts instead of putting too much trust in the government. Thus it begs the question: How much is too much? How often are liberals willing to depend upon the government to tell them that snakes don't need oiling? Isn't it just as dangerous for the government to gain all the trust as it is for a consumer in a market to trust a seller without verification?

Those who want to put all their faith in government will have to understand that people have different ideas about what's valuable to them. And individuals have to be free to learn from their mistakes. Has anyone really ever oiled a snake? The point is that we will all make bad purchases in our lifetime as consumers. Capitalism and a free market are not perfect because people are not perfect. There is some oversight needed and some regulations do need to be governmentally controlled. But people making decisions based upon logic would rarely make a bad purchase twice.

Too much government regulation, however, may force people into a zombie-like state of trust in everything in their world based upon their trust in government. A free market allows people to make mistakes. It works pretty well because most people value their time and their purchases. If individuals outsource their trust to someone or something else, it takes away their ability to figure out for themselves whether or not snakes need oil. And if they can't figure that out for themselves, they can be convinced of just about anything.

Moving Forward

From this point in the book forward I am going to begin the process of applying conservatism and logic to some modern-day political issues. I will tackle what I perceive to be the most contentious and/or talked about issues of our time. The goal will be to get the reader to understand them the way I do; if they do not already. Unfortunately, I can't write about every political issue there is because there simply is not enough time. This book, as I've stated, will not be a mammoth. Let's say we'll make it as long as necessary and as short as possible. Thus, the issues will generally be the more distinguishable and easily noticed. My hope is that at the end of the book, logic and conservatism will either make sense or make even more sense. If this book only works to irritate the reader, then they are too far skewed to the left and their only relief may come from a long swim…to Cuba!!

Chapter 5
Abortion

One of the most contentious political issues of the last 50 years is the issue of abortion and when human life begins. It's appropriate, therefore, to start off the "issues" section of the book with abortion and why conservatives, even the under-religious ones, view abortion in the same light as ending any human life; which is to say that it's wrong. Thus far I've built up the definition of conservatism like a pyramid so I think it's best to apply it to perhaps one of the most recognizable and polarizing issues the country has ever dealt with.

Another good reason to begin with abortion is because at first glance, the average apolitical or liberal person might be quick to call conservatives hypocrites when it comes to the issue of abortion. An anti-abortion stance requires one to demand that abortion be an illegal act; which means that the government would be prohibiting a woman from undergoing what some consider a simple medical procedure. Liberals like to proclaim this as an inconsistency or juxtaposition of the issue of government overreach and a conservative's natural inclination toward less government in general. The essence of anti-abortion laws is in fact government outlawing this procedure. But there is no contradiction on the part of conservatives over this issue because it's logical for a society to have a clear definition of when life begins. This ensures that civilized people will not be arbitrarily ending human lives; which is hard to argue in favor of.

Let's examine why it is that conservatives are pro-life, based upon logic. There are many religious views that create a natural disdain for abortion. These are based on the spiritual essence of the human soul that religion promotes. But logic, combined with a view of human life as a precious commodity, should lead everyone to the same conclusion about the misguided rhetoric regarding abortion. One doesn't have to be a religious person to understand love or the uniqueness of the human species. Viewing abortion as the ending a life should transcend into the secular world as well.

If abortion were truly just a simple medical procedure, then no conservative would argue against a women's right to choose to have one performed. If the government was to prohibit a medical procedure arbitrarily it would be a genuine abuse of power. There is, however, a much bigger issue at stake than a simple medical procedure; that is when life begins.

One would have to assume that most people who claim to be pro-choice, and thus do not believe abortion should be illegal, don't necessarily think that life begins at the time of conception. That would seemingly be the only way one could justify the position of pro-choice. It's an easy way to acquit oneself from having to decide when life begins or, more importantly, having to endure the burden of guilt over ending a life. To hold the belief that an embryo is not a human life is a way to keep the procedure "scientific," thus making it seem more like a routine medical procedure. Hence, the decision is made with a doctor and it's no different than a nose-job or breast enlargement; both of which are cosmetic and personal medical decisions.

Before I proceed further let me clarify a misconception about conservatives and the conception argument to life: we don't hate or think ill of women who have had the abortion procedure done. The conclusions we draw are our own, though the hope is that others will eventually be convinced to see it the same. Women who have undergone the procedure are not enemies nor do conservatives think that they don't appreciate the sanctity of life.

Unfortunately a lot of liberal mouthpieces would have women thinking otherwise. It's true that conservatives do not like the procedure because of our logical assumptions and feelings about when life begins, but we also understand that the notion of pregnancy versus when life begins is a very socially vague concept. The hope is that going forward, conservatives can work to advance the logical conclusion that life begins at conception. And perhaps someday all people will come to understand and develop an appreciation for the smallest of human lives.

Most conservatives are pro-life because the logical conclusion is that life begins at the point of conception. Any attempt to conclude otherwise is an effort to shield oneself from logic and again, more importantly, guilt. A person has to truly stretch their conscience trying to reason differently because arguing any other point along the line of pregnancy, as to when life begins, is speculative and arbitrary. There may be no better argument for 4 months than there is for 6.

The exact point could seemingly be different for every person; and that would extend to persons in the medical field as well. If life's beginning is not at conception then the beginning is open to interpretation, which is a ridiculous notion. And although conception does not always naturally manifest into human life, due to reasons we are sometimes at a loss to explain, it's how every life begins; regardless of how long it lasts. Thus, we can't use the excuse that conception doesn't always equal life to justifiably end it in the womb; otherwise every natural death could be justification for ending a life early.

The fact remains there is no official scientific starting point to human life that has any medical consensus with the exception of birth. Of course, basing it on birth is unjustifiable since there have been many humans born prematurely who have survived to live long and healthy lives. Thus, the only other point along the pregnancy trail that has continuity to all pregnancies is conception. It truly is the "starting point" to all human life. For one to argue that conception is not the beginning of life they must then positively pinpoint a stage of embryonic development which does. Some may say it's when the eyes develop, and others may say it's when the heart begins to beat; which begins very soon into pregnancy. There could be perhaps thousands of interpretations trying to identify at what stage of pregnancy life really begins.

Logic has to dictate that life begins at conception because it's the only true point that every pregnancy shares, regardless of how far into the developmental process the fetus makes it. The problem is many people want to intentionally keep the question of when life begins ambiguous and vague for the purpose of allowing people to choose convenience over personal responsibility. It's the admission that conception equals life, or the conscious part of pregnancy, that people must come to terms with. As an intelligent and reasoning species we can't have multiple definitions and overlapping opinions about what part of pregnancy a life actually becomes worthy of birth. That's not very cool.

Galactic Accident?

When delving into a topic that deals with the spirit and uniqueness of human life, we have to ask the question whether or not the human life is indeed special. That's where the real answer to the question of whether abortion is a justifiable option will be ultimately be answered. Most people would probably agree that there is a particular uncommonness about humans that sets us exclusively apart from any other life forms we find on Earth. Even to the non-religious persons, the human experience has got to be seen as something very different in comparison to other life forms. I'd argue what separates us most from all other species of life, aside from greater intelligence, is the fact that humans have emotions that don't appear to impact other mammals and animals to the extent they do us.

When it comes to survival and the inherent longing to live, which all species have to some degree, humans indeed share many traits with the animal kingdom. For example, attributes such as fear, which tends to keep us out of danger, is something necessary to survive. As well, fight, flight, sleepiness and playfulness are all somewhat shared traits. These all contribute to the sense of self-preservation that most living things possess. However, humans have a degree of emotion and self-awareness that doesn't exist in the animal kingdom and, as well, doesn't seem to have any real advantages toward human durability and survival.

For example, humans feel sadness and depression which can translate to tears and prolonged feelings of apathy. We also experience joy to the extent of laughter, which may also bring on tears. Even such subtle swings of emotion from grumpy to cheerful, separate us from other species which tend to stay more static with their emotions; concentrating almost exclusively on those characteristics pertaining to survival. Deep human emotion has no lasting quality as a means of self-preservation. In other words, when looked at scientifically, this kind of emotion has no real survival value. So, we ask, why does it exist?

There are definitive comparisons to be made and examples to cite in which the animal kingdom can exhibit emotion, but those are generally not sustained over time the way human emotion is. Humans on the other hand have the gift of real and lingering emotion; depending on one's mood…the gift or curse perhaps. Nonetheless it's the kind of emotion that can bring a smile to someone's face years after the initial emotion was felt.

This is the kind of emotion that allows us to feel deep love and true hatred. It is unique to the human species. Some may say it is a byproduct of a high intelligence, but then one must ask, why only us? Why only one species with massive intelligence compared to all other species? Many species, outside of humans, have comparable intelligence to one another. If it were truly a game of constantly evolving intelligence, then we could assume there would be many intelligent species. But there is only one.

There are varying degrees of intelligence in the animal kingdom, but human intelligence dwarfs all others by comparison. Humans also have a unique level of emotions. Of course it's important to distinguish this emotion from that which is the characteristic driving the emotional liberal to be trusting and dependent upon a central government. Within the spectrum of human emotions, liberals tend to gravitate to the overreacting and distraught passions; thus being guided politically to draw conclusions based on emotion.

It's important to acknowledge real human emotion as a unique and deeply personal human quality, but something that can be differentiated in governance. Love, respect and adoration are qualities that humans have and generally we understand these make us special. Conservatives understand that we must cherish such unique emotions as well, but that the community as a whole cannot be guided by agitation or frenzy masked as emotion. Rather the whole must embrace pure pragmatism and logic in governance. Despite these strong emotions, humans have the ability to distinguish.

Some might believe that this human uniqueness is the odd byproduct of a larger galactic accident. These people may or may not choose to believe in any number of scientific explanations as to the origins of the Earth such as the Big Bang Theory. This would embrace the notion of an enormous space explosion that saw the Earth end up in just the right spot, in reference to the sun, to support life. If that is the case, they may simply view humans as the winners in the development game; beings with the brains and body structure to rule the planet. This planetary placement means that life can only exist when certain very specific conditions are met. If these conditions are not met, then it's either too hot, too cold or there's not enough of something to support life.

But really, that's a hard conclusion to draw considering the vast array of life and life adaptations we see right here on Earth. If this planet isn't special then why can't there be life on other planets? There are many different forms of life on Earth that survive and thrive in unique ways in varying geographical scenarios. Some life forms need far less of certain Earthly attributes that others need far more of. So again we ask, why couldn't life exist on other planets in our solar system where there is far more or far less of what is here on Earth?

Nobody is truly certain as to what is the actual "backbone" for life to exist. Some think it's H2O but there is no real way to be certain of that. Science may use the model of Earth and apply it to other planets to draw that conclusion, but that's just an attempt to use science explain what seems unexplainable about life on Earth. There really is no actual scientific formula for life, except for what we know about life on Earth; thus this place could indeed be special.

If we can conclude one way or another that life here is special and the starting point was at conception for all living beings, then we simply cannot justify abortion. Every person was once at the conception stage. Science may try to be slick in its explanations that humans are just a space accident; thus no soul. But for those who believe in the legality of abortion, they need to take time to think about their humanness.

They need to take time to look around and notice that this place does have uniqueness, whether through creation or not. Perhaps they need to ask themselves if they're willing to accept the fact that they, and everyone they love, are indeed the result of a gigantic galactic coincidence. Not everyone must be religious to understand this point about Earth and its special-ness. But if one understands it and their starting point was at conception, then it's safe to say that abortion is the end to what could be someone else's specialness.

Unwanted Pregnancies

Despite the arguments about when life "scientifically" begins and whether a fetus is human, there are, in fact, opinions and justifications for legal abortion which disregard completely any scientific rationale; and they don't really account for human emotion either. Rather they are based solely on convenience; and these are the worst kind of justifications. It is the argument which dehumanizes our senses. The argument is this: some proponents will justify abortion by making a woman's pregnancy out to be a matter of convenience in deciding whether or not a baby should be born. It's perhaps one of the arguments we hear most often when supporters of abortion opine about the right of a woman to choose to have an abortion or not.

The intentional vagueness about when life scientifically begins for proponents of abortion can be a justification for the larger issue of whether or not the mother or parents feel they have the time or capacity to raise the child the woman finds herself carrying. Using the "unwanted pregnancy" excuse is a way to shift blame from the sexual activity of the parents to the unwanted conception of the sperm and egg. In other words, it's not the adults having sex to blame for the pregnancy, it's that whole reproduction pro-cess thingy.

The argument is made countless times from abortion supporters that if society were to make abortion an illegal act, then there will be endless unwanted pregnancies ending in millions of children growing up in undesirable conditions. Therefore, in some cases, they'd argue abortion is saving a child and mother from a situation that neither wants nor would want to be in. And to be slick about it, liberals will often use fiscal responsibility against conservatives to make the argument.

They will say that the "state" (synonymous with the government at any level) will be saving money because most of these pregnancies happen to women who cannot afford to have a child, and if they do, they will become a financial burden on the tax payers of the community. That reasoning, however, is void of reason. Societies simply cannot validate ending a life based upon the potential it has to be mistreated or undervalued by the carrier or the family in which it would become a part of. That's not very cool.

As humans we attempt to "play God," if you will, when we allow abortion to be justified by the convenience value of that life against the current responsibility level the parents are willing to endure. There really is no way to argue in favor of making a decision about the importance of a life before that life has begun. Yet abortion, based on convenience, does just that. It places little value on the potential of that human life and shifts the value in favor of the parent's current lifestyle.

These potential people haven't yet had the chance to prove themselves worthy or unworthy of existing alongside the rest of humanity. Thus another question must be asked: who are "we" to decide whether a person gets a chance at life or not? Abortion takes away the opportunity for this same life that appears to have intrinsic value to the vast majority of humans that are born. To base the decision of ending a life in the womb on the timing of the pregnancy and whether it's a convenient time in the parent's life for a child is a very sick and disturbing attitude for society to allow.

This particular argument would have a better chance at validity, though perhaps not justification, if we as humans didn't understand how life is procreated. But the fact remains that we do know how babies are made and in almost every instance of conception it's the act of sex which allows for that. If folklore held true and there were storks delivering babies to front door steps around the world, then one could see the validity in refusing delivery. What some may consider a blessing, others may not want to burden themselves with at the present time. This accidental delivery would not justify death to the child, but perhaps delivery to another address. But the truth is that sex is a chosen activity, mostly, and one in which we as humans understand the potential outcomes of. It's the act of two, or more, people having sexual relations which could potentially contribute to the "unwanted pregnancy."

If we analyze the statement "unwanted pregnancy" we will understand that it is both an exaggeration of terms and oxymoronic in its phraseology.

To call a pregnancy unwanted is akin to calling the sensation of feeling full an "unwanted satiation." One could imagine the ridicule they would have bestowed upon them if they were to eat six pieces of pizza and then complain that they have an irrational sense of being full from eating. Thus, it may be an unwanted sensation but one brought about by cognizant actions.

To be sure, if one did not "want" this feeling, there were measures that could have been taken long before the sixth piece of pizza were eaten. The gluttony, as well as the pregnancy, is more an inconvenient truth than an inadvertent outcome. As a society of persons who value our existence, we can't allow the impulsiveness of sexual activity to justify ending life. To say it differently, we who cherish life cannot characterize its beginning as mistaken, regardless of how unplanned it may be. That, as well, isn't very cool.

To reiterate, the debate about abortion and convenience in terms of choice leaves out the idea of people acting responsibly to begin with. This argument has no doubt trickled down to our society's youth and infiltrated their sense of sex and reasonable expectations. More and more sexual activity is being accepted as a happening and not as a decision; thus creating a rationalization for making the abortion option available. Too often adults will use the erratic and unpredictable tendencies of youth to defend the abortion option based on convenience. But to allow the excuse that there is little that can be done about teen sex as a justification for making abortion an option is irresponsible and dutifully lazy on the part of adults. When children and teens are cared for and taught appropriately they tend to understand and heed advice.

There are, however, some terrible and unworthy parents of children and teens. Some children come from unspeakably bad predicaments in their upbringing and as a result they have little concept of responsibility and reason. Nonetheless, as a society we simply perpetuate a cycle of irresponsibility on the part of these young people by allowing abortion to be an option for unwanted pregnancies. Teens that come from bad environments need more reason to understand the specialness of human life and not reinforcement in its devaluation based on convenience. As a society of people who generally understand the concept of human specialness, I would argue that we have the obligation to advance that notion in an effort to live more fulfilling lives.

In A Dark Alley

Proponents of abortion have a multitude of justifications they'll deploy in an effort to ensure what they call a woman's "reproductive rights" are upheld. Thus far I have pointed out the hypocrisy of abortion based upon the viewpoints which undervalue the human spirit as well as those that place a higher importance on an egocentric personal existence. But there's yet another reason supporters of abortion have for keeping it legal; that it ensures women's safety. There are those who will argue that in the absence of legal and medically overseen abortion women will attempt to perform it on their own and inadvertently cause bodily harm to themselves.

That way of thinking, though perhaps placing value on the life of the woman, again removes the concept of personal responsibility long before the decision to self operate was made. The dark alley reference parodies the sense of being alone and a feeling of helplessness on the part of the pregnant woman as she performs the abortion on herself; even if indeed she were physically in a dark alley. This kind of personal medical infliction has been performed by women in the past with objects such as coat hangers and other long or sharp devices and has consequently ended with severe and life-threatening damage to the mother. But again…that's not the unborn child's fault.

To say that society ought to keep abortion legal because women will potentially harm themselves by attempting to abort the baby themselves or having it done under less than medical conditions removes the larger picture. The pregnancy, unplanned or not, started with the decision to have sexual relations. Most people can recall their high school science class in which they learned the concept that "every action has an equal or greater reaction." If having sex is the action my guess would be that orgasm is the equal, but pregnancy the greater. It's not as though this concept of sex potentially leading to pregnancy is a new discovery. In a society of special beings, abortion allows us to excuse our intentional and knowledge-able behavior, favoring convenience over life. And that's not cool.

Conservatives are not naïve however. We do understand that abortion, the procedure and the psychological effects, can be a trigger of personal devastation for some women. Our stance against abortion does not, by any means, conclude that women who have had the procedure done are somehow evil villains. They're not. The majority of abortions are done on younger women who may not have had the life experiences to understand how precious and how fragile life can be. Coupled with the societal acceptance of abortion as a simple medical procedure, it's no wonder younger women-and some men for that matter- will accept the procedure despite the potential emotional risks.

Abortion is really an issue about life and not a political issue about women's rights. Many liberal women-and some men- would scoff at that notion but as far as conservatives are concerned, that's the issue. It's not just a simple medical procedure; it's a procedure that stops a potential human life in motion. Every person we see was begun at conception. It's not a matter of choice versus anti-choice because the real choice begins with the one to have sex. Though gratifying for sure, sex has implications and a purpose beyond the sensational. This is especially important when it involves the understanding by the country's youth. It's important to teach the youth that life is not expendable simply because it hasn't reached the stage of development to make decisions for itself. And life should not be devalued to the extent that it's referred to in terms of convenience. That's terribly un-cool.

Rape

When the issue of abortion is talked about, one must consider that a small number of pregnancies happen in the instance of sexual rape. Liberals will attempt to pin conservatives into a corner over the issue of rape and how it pertains to abortion rights. Despite their efforts, there is but one conclusion that a logical person can make in the instances of pregnancy and rape; the women must be given the opportunity to decide to continue or not continue the pregnancy. No matter one's belief in regard to the human spirit and the specialness of our being, as a society we cannot expect a woman whose been forcibly impregnated to carry out. If abortion were outlawed, with this exception, no logical conservative would argue against it.

That being said, if abortion were illegal with this exception, the offense would obviously require medical examination. That's not to say that anyone would lie about rape, but young people may get scared if they feel like they've made a life altering choice without means to support it. But to protect them and the innocence of life, verification would have to be done and done quickly. Any conservative who tries to tie in rape and pregnancy to their religious beliefs by means of divinity, is simply not being practical. Though one may believe the life created as a consequence of a rape is still purposeful, as a society we need to stick with logical conclusions for the victims. Perhaps adding manslaughter to the charge of rape in the case of pregnancy would be appropriate.

Chapter 6
Racism

When measuring political issues on the sensitivity scale, going from abortion to race relations is like jumping out of the frying pan and into the fire. As if abortion as an issue were not emotional enough, let's delve into the politicization of race in America. History has made race relations in America an issue, but emotional people (overreacting people) have done their best to keep the issue from progressing toward a harmonious end. The United States has had an ugly history when it comes to dealing with race. For that matter, the world has had an ugly history when dealing with racial differences. It certainly is hard to imagine a time when race was not just a hot-button political issue but rather a societal definition as to what, not who, a person is.

Race relations have become a political issue in America because it took politics to change what was an injustice in regard to how blacks and other minorities were not recognized by the government the way whites were. Most people are no doubt aware that the United States government used to treat and recognize people differently based upon their race. In essence it meant that some people were guaranteed the protection of their rights as a citizen while others were not. Even post Civil War, which was a war to preserve the Union and unify the country, it took many generations before blacks and others would see the day they were considered truly equal under the law.

For a long time, the government did not recognize non-whites the way it did white people. There were separate sets of rules governing the different races. Socially it was acceptable to consider "colored" folks different and not deserving of basic accommodations that were afforded to white folks. The government disallowed basic privileges to minorities by way of defining them as inferior to white people. One could make the argument that it was government reacting to the sentiments of the era but perhaps it was vice versa. Maybe the folks in government were helping to prolong the negative attitudes and bias toward minority persons. Nonetheless, it has taken America a long time to evolve into a truly tolerant and equal society.

In modern times, people in the media and those whose liberalism is fraught with anger have tried to pin the lingering negative racial sentiments on conservatives and/or Republicans. They do this to stir up emotions and cause rage, but they are aware that the notion of racism being a conservative attribute is ridiculous. However, if they can shout loud enough there are some people who will begin to believe that to be true. As adversaries of the conservative view of logic and limited government, they have one really strong tool…hyperbole; and they use it in an effort to verbally trademark conservatives so as to gain support from those who will consider such nonsense to be true.

People who harbor racist views have nothing in common with the way in which conservative's view everyone's equal opportunity in this country. As it is, their logic for labeling conservatives as racist is to apply the word "conservative" to a reactionary viewpoint that finds solace in the past. In other words, they try to make people think that conservatives long for the convictions of the past when whites were deemed superior.

But when one understands the core of the conservative philosophy, they will see that this cannot be the case. It would be oxymoronic as it would go against the conservative's basic feelings about life, justice, equality and personal responsibility. Not to mention that it would imply that black conservatives in modern times have a desire to return to their status as subordinate citizen; ridiculous indeed.

The reality is that minorities, blacks especially, were treated very poorly for a long time and some of the negative effects of that still exist today, though in much smaller amounts. For white people to proliferate the feelings of racism toward minorities means that somewhere, someone has failed them. Conversely, minorities who feel that they have a right to be racist toward whites as a form of ancestral retribution are clueless as well. The fact is that the ugliest part of racism existed in America in a time which no longer has any living witnesses. There are accounts and descriptions but those people have all since passed. Thus, the folks who still feel it necessary to carry on racist traditions or pretend to feel the struggles of the past need to move on.

Is Racism Real?

Allow me to make a bold statement and say that racism, by definition, simply cannot be real. It truly can't be possible to hate a person based solely upon the individual's racial make-up. That kind of hate is transparent and is usually the result of a person's upbringing or misguided culture. People who profess to be racist by way of slurs, slogans or rituals don't really hate people because they are different from them racially; they simply have been led to think that they do.

Stereotypes are not an easy thing to overcome and even harder to overlook. If someone has been surrounded by racist ideas from an early age, then they will most certainly carry those notions into adulthood. Occasionally these subside and rational people triumph, but not all do. It's one thing for people to make light of race to point out the absurdity of racism, but when persons allow hate to manifest into mistreatment it becomes ridiculous.

When one thinks about racism logically they will understand that no one can truly hate another person based on their race alone, without even knowing them.

Imagine a psychological study, if you will, which is conducted under preset conditions. If five individuals of differing races were placed into a large room with dividers so that they cannot see one another, could they hate the person on the other side of the divider based on race? Perhaps they can hear each other and converse, which may produce kinships or enemies, but they cannot see one another. If the study were conducted over a one week period we could expect the participants would get to know one another. If at the end of the experiment, and upon meeting the person on the other side of the divider, any of the participants suddenly decided they hated one person because of their race it would be transparent indeed. Thus racism is a contrived notion and not real.

Does a Person's Race Matter?

When thinking about a group or community of people, does an individual's race truly matter in regard to how anybody should be accepted? People generally understand that not all individuals look the same in terms of genetic make-up. Some people have darker skin, some have darker hair, others have lighter skin and even facial structure will vary slightly depending upon race. Even among people of the same race there can be stark differences in skin tone, hair color, eye shape and so on. Again, we ask: Does that matter?

Perhaps the answer is to that question is…maybe. Race only matters insofar as it matters to an individual, because a person's race only accounts for a small percentage of the difference between people. People are more likely to find similarities and develop relation-ships based upon their values than they are to simply migrate to other persons based on race. Those char-acteristics are important to identify because, unlike liberalism which generally puts people into groups based on appearance, it helps break down stereotypes and misguided notions of race.

One might ask, however: Doesn't being around people who share our unique racial make-up create a sense of belonging and a certain comfort level? The answer to that might also be….maybe. Ultimately that would be up to the individual, but in society we do often see groups of people in assembly and congregating together into churches, neighborhoods, etc… base upon race. It doesn't mean they harbor racist thoughts; it most likely is just a reaction to the fact that persons in the company of others who share their racial make-up may find it easier not having to think about how they might differ from a larger group. Thus, black churches or Hispanic neighborhoods, as examples, make sense and it's OK. Socially speak-ing, people can usually figure out what makes them comfortable and weed out the bad seeds. What they do not need are persons in government constantly sounding an alarm bell about racism.

Conservatism, due to its core belief in the power of the individual, embodies the opinion that everybody has the capability to become a great individual. Like-wise, it's understood that anyone can succumb to ste-reotyping if they are not strong willed enough. Race only plays a part in shaping individuals if a group of people are led to believe that something about their race's mental or physical makeup is starkly different; either for better or worse. But thankfully it's generally accepted that American society has moved past that. The next step is for liberalism to move past stereotyping conservatives as racist because we disagree with their ideology as a whole.

Government Action

In the U.S. it took a long time for blacks and other minorities to obtain their just rights. It is astonishing to try to understand the attitudes toward minorities when one looks back in time through a modern prism. With a clearer understanding of the value of all human life today, it's ridiculous for any person to continue to harbor thoughts of racial inequality. When it was government as a body which adhered to these sentiments, it was ultimately cruel and unjust. The U.S. government, however, was finally pressured, from the outside in, to legally change what was changing in American society already. The call for Civil Rights in the 1960's was government finally coming around to the changes the country was in need of. But logical people would question some of the programs that politicians embarked on in an effort to retrospectively correct their injustices.

There's no doubt that Civil Rights legislation of the 1960's was needed to "right the ship" as it pertained to the government's treatment of minorities. Minorities had earned their rights with the victory of the North in the Civil War, some hundred years prior, but the social mistreatment was still tolerated by government and others. The social tides had been surging for a long time prior and change finally washed ashore. Hence, legislation was passed that gave blacks and others civil rights under the Constitution; much to the dismay of many southern Democratic politicians.

After so many generations of people believing that government sponsored inequality against minorities was valid, there's no doubt the road ahead was going to be difficult. They had to overcome discrimination that government policies helped to manifest by legally allowing such things as separate bathrooms, drinking fountains and even seating on busses for "colored" persons. But could it be argued that government intervention into the integration process was an attempt at atonement which only further complicated the racial sentiments?

Government policies such as Affirmative Action were put in place in an effort to aid the integration process of black Americans into being accepted in the workplace in what was traditionally a segregated environment. In essence, it required government employers, and some doing business with the government, to hire a particular percentage of minorities as part of their overall workforce. There were other facets to the integration process, but Affirmative Action was perhaps the biggest. It's no doubt true that most Americans were ready to proceed with the Civil Rights legislation, but were they prepared to shoulder the responsibilities and facilitate the corrections the government was trying to make?

The U.S. government kept antiquated policies in place dividing the races, long after they should have been discontinued. With the creation of Affirmative Action it subsequently forced hiring decisions to be made based on…race. One can see the irony involved and perhaps understand the ire of some people over Affirmative Action. That government enabled discrimination for so long and then attempted to correct it by allowing discrimination is laughable. That's not to say that employers wouldn't hire minority candidates, but if certain qualifications were absent, then it makes no sense to have to fill a quota because public policy was fumbled for so long. Conservatives don't argue against such policies to be contrarian but rather because when one thinks about a solution to the integration process, that type of solution doesn't seem logical.

Were there inequalities, fostered by stereotypes, which would have to be rethought? The answer was and is: Yes. And the government's prior policy guidelines involving race were going to make the transition to an equal society difficult. But mandating hiring quotas simply means that qualified persons would be overlooked based upon race. It's difficult to fight discrimination while discriminating, which is what the attempt was with Affirmative Action. That's not to say that everything that resulted from Affirmative Action was necessarily negative, however, in theory it's antagonistic. It would seem to perpetuate the idea that race is a guideline.

Perhaps with a new found freedom, blacks and

other minority groups would have flourished in society despite government attempting to manipulate the integration process. But again it would be intention triumphing over philosophy and results. Black Americans earned their freedom the hard way with much pride and determination. Some government help was to be necessary in the desegregation process for sure, but my guess is that pride would have given blacks and other minorities the recognition as humans and citizens regardless of any quota system. One could argue that Affirmative Action policies have actually slowed the achievement process for minorities the same way any government social program might. It takes away incentive, building on the notion that the government will equalize outcomes. Discrimination is a terrible thing and every American can be thankful that those policies are now in the past.

The race to characterize people as racists is repugnant and insane. Conservatives are usually the more color blind of the people I know in terms of judging by character and not labeling people as part of a group based on what they look like. We, as conservatives, are also much less offended by racial misjudgments others may produce and we're less prone to the emotional stirrings of race baiters. I draw that conclusion because conservatives don't see a need to group people based on race. Two persons of the same race can be, and usually are, vastly different human beings. Liberal bureaucrats are in love with the idea of racial make-up. So much so that they feel a need to categorize Americans every ten years with the Census by requiring a racial identification be made. There's no logical reason the government should care what a person's cultural background is. There' no benefit to it, it's not cool and it only further perpetuates the stigma that people are different based on race. The government should not be in the business of race recognition.

Chapter 7
Public Spending

The American government has the authority to tax citizens with the understanding that the communal collection of money be used in the most logical and practical way possible to facilitate public entities. In other words, the government should spend money it collects in taxes on services that the private sector can't reasonably be expected to fairly maintain. That being said, the government spends a lot of money on things that the private sector would never touch because there is no real demand for it. Elected officials, however, will use money collected on taxes and fees to fund silly ideas they have about how a social network of people should live. It's not always the most logical or practical, but they believe there's a need so citizens often get handed public services that do not need to exist.

Public spending, like many things in life, is beautiful only in the eyes of the beholders. Thus, bad spending can be justified if bureaucrats can convince other bureaucrats that there is even a modicum of necessity to the funding in question. This is why it's terribly important to elect officials who do not view the public trough of revenue as a magic pot of gold that can be dipped into for frivolous public projects. The citizens expect the government folks to view that money as hard earned by the tax payers and treat the spending of it with a sense of pride. People put in long and hard hours for money that gets spent on some very questionable government ventures.

Public spending of tax payer money should always be done with much deliberation and adherence to what's logical. Bad habits have developed in government to the extent that in many cities, counties, states and at the federal level the amount of impractical spending has led to enormous debts. The overall spending the government does needs to be drastically reduced because it can. Too much money is wasted at the government level and that is accounting for generational debt to be passed on.

Politicians must fail to realize that an economy ebbs and flows, through good times and bad. If they do understand this concept then they are ignoring it at the expense of the citizens. During economic growth periods the government generally sees an uptick in tax revenue that comes in because economic growth means the people are making more money. Unfortunately, it's times like these in which elected officials who are in charge of spending and budgeting tend to create more government projects because there is a surplus of money. However when the economy trends downward for a period of time, they have a big problem because this will now cause a shortfall in funding of the projects started during boom times.

The truth is that there will always be enough money to fund the basic and logical functions of government. It comes down to eliminating the useless and illogical projects and handouts that tend to suck the revenue dry. There is a major difference in philosophy between conservatives and liberals when it comes to public spending. Just because money is available to the government, it does not mean that it must be spent. Funding that is unnecessary is money that should come back to the tax payer. True conservative politicians understand that concept and do not look to constantly create more government entities and dependents.

Liberal politicians need a perspective change as it pertains to government spending. Just because it is government doing the spending does not mean it's advisable or even practical. This does not mean, however, that conservative politicians are in favor of eliminating all things which are government funded. Funding for public parks, pools and other development does not need to disappear. The people should simply demand that logic dictate the levels of government spending. There are many people holding public positions who are persuaded to spend money unwisely and oversight is hard to employ. A conservative, however, naturally understands what unnecessary spending looks like; objectivity in government is not a difficult thing.

Government Money

It's important to remember that the government does not really have any money. The money that it spends on road work, police and fire, and military comes primarily from taxes and fees collected on the citizens. The aforementioned public entities can be seen as examples of the government spending tax money logically and objectively. The road system, in a society that depends on the vehicle as much as Americans do, is not something that can be reasonably managed by the private sector. Much to the dismay of bicyclists, the vehicle is what Americans depend upon.

A public road system is logical because it allows everyone access to the roads and does not restrict access for private market reasons such as non-payment of fees. One can imagine a fully privatized road system in which sections of streets and towns were divided up amongst private firms and how that would be impractical. It might require multiple checkpoint stops for verification of payment; each company no doubt employing a different method by which to verify. That type of system does not seem logical. Thus, spending tax revenue on a public road system makes good and practical sense.

The same type of reasoning could extend to the justification of a publicly funded police force and fire and rescue team. A system of private police would fall short of its mission because the decision to respond to an emergency might end up being based on a credit score. That, again, is not logical. Public spending does play an essential role in the United States in that it fills the holes of logical services that a market economy cannot reasonably be expected to fill. One can probably think of a number of things that are financed by public dollars; some are reasonable and some are plain ridiculous.

In the next segment of the book, I want to delve into a few publicly funded entities and give my reasoning as to why they either should not exist or need to be scaled back immensely. It's certainly one man's opinion, but I want the reader to understand that government officials need to constantly be aware that the money they spend belongs to the people who pay taxes. They only get to spend it because the tax payers allow them to. The question must always be asked: "what is a reasonable way for government to spend collected tax money?"

At first glance one may think that most entities that are publicly financed have a need they are fulfilling outside of the demands of the private market; and that may be true. But just because they do, does not make them necessary. Some citizens may gloss over the fact that certain programs need not exist simply because they've existed for such a long time. Perhaps they seem to be as much a part of everyday life for citizens as the road systems or police and fire. However, many government bodies or programs can be scaled back and do not need the massive amount of funding they absorb. Some of these institutes and services may seem untouchable to the average voter, but they shouldn't. And in many cases it would be really cool if they went through a logical reconstruction.

Public Spending Reduction: Transportation

Public transportation is a prime example of a government service which seems to be both untouchable, due to its longevity as a service, and its appearance as a private market void-filler. Personally, I have no idea when or where the idea of public transportation originated and what the initial logic was behind it; and I mentioned I won't be doing much research. But in my opinion, it has given the green light (pun intended) to bolster the public bureaucracy of transportation to a size that is not reasonable. Prior to the attainability of a personal vehicle for most consumers, the trolley car probably seemed like a logical way to spend some public money. It no doubt was a driver (pun) of economic activity in growing cities and thus probably paid for itself in terms of tax revenue created by the commerce it helped manifest. But in today's America is that need still there?

In modern day America, most citizens use their own method of personal transportation via a car or motorcycle or bicycle. Very few people depend on public transportation as their primary method of transit. So let me start there: the "who" of public transportation. As a percentage of the public, there are very few persons who do not have the means or ability to obtain a vehicle, bicycle or shoes for that matter. Thus, the majority of persons who ride the bus or train do so because they choose to budget the expenses of personal vehicles out of their lives or limit what they spend on maintenance and gas. Whether that reason is financial or because they work in a downtown metropolis where the government has intentionally limited the parking available, they are choosing to use the bus or train.

The majority of the use, however, is from people who choose to use it because it is cheaper than operating a personal vehicle (gas, insurance, maintenance, etc.). Thus we can conclude that the government has developed, and subsequently greatly enhanced, a system of transportation primarily for a group of persons they assume cannot afford to buy a car. But, we must ask, how many of those people would budget differently and purchase even a cheap vehicle if there were no busses? The answer is that probably a majority of them would. In the absence of public transportation, or at least in the excessive form most cities develop it today, people would find a way to get around.

Let's also ask the question: does having such a vast public transportation system make people more or less self reliant? As well, is it the duty of the government, logically, to provide free or cheap methods of transportation? To many conservatives, that doesn't seem like a logical way to spend millions of dollars. It feels more like the bureaucrats are creating the need to substantiate the necessity. It's one thing for the government to be the developer of the road system itself, but to provide the method of transport for some is quite different.

Perhaps some would argue that the public transportation system is paid for by its riders and thus is not a financial burden on those who choose not to ride. That argument, however, is not true by a long shot. It's accurate to say that the fees the busses and trains charge is applied to the cost of operation but the majority of the cost is supplied by those who do not ride. Taxes on items such as car tires, gas and other local fees are extracted from taxpayers to pay for public transportation. That should be pretty obvious considering the relatively inexpensive fares coupled with the frequency with which the bus has empty seats.

In essence public transportation is being continually funded and expanded to be beneficial to a very small group of people. It has ballooned to modern day proportions because there are now people who have developed a lifestyle around public transportation. Thus, the growth has simply become that of the frequency of operation and it is not meeting realistic economic goals. It has, in fact, become a staple of our society so there is probably no real possibility of eliminating it completely. But, if the government is going to maintain the busses and trains and hire those who will drive them, wouldn't it seem to make sense that those who ride should cover the bulk of the cost, if not all of it?

The cost factor is perhaps the biggest reason that most logical people don't like to see the public transportation system operating at the levels it does. When it is as large as it is, it means that a lot of taxpayer money is going in to fund it. And it can't be an inexpensive operation. Conservatives generally don't think that having non-riders pay for what is primarily used by a small group of people makes sense. Taxing business in an effort to fund the bus is not fair either. Local bureaucrats, however, enact laws that justify taxing business owners for public transit as an "operating cost" of doing business in a community. But using that logic would imply the same should be true for all commuters regardless of whether they use public transportation or not. Of course, that's not logical either.

We need to remember that the government chooses to provide this service and is by no means obligated. The question should be asked: is it logical to fund public transportation at the levels that some cities in America do today? Not everybody can ride the bus, as there are simply not enough busses or trains to accommodate the community as a whole. Yet we allow for government to operate a system which grants some people the opportunity to budget a vehicle out of their lives.

It turns the idea of public transit into a humanitarian effort. The emotion of the issue forbids some liberals to get past the idea that the bus is available for the poor and the elderly. If we succumb to that notion then we, as a community, must learn to operate the system at a smaller and more cost effective level. It simply makes sense that those who ride should absorb most of the cost and that can be achieved by limiting the operation; thus keeping fare prices lower.

Large metropolis areas often see ridership at higher levels than do moderate sized cities and in those cases it may make sense to provide it at such a rate to reach demand. Of course the demand is often skewed due to downtown zoning which often doesn't allow for the amount of parking structures to exist which would accommodate the traffic. Nonetheless, if it alleviates a potential traffic problem, in a highly condensed area of commerce, then perhaps there may be some value and logic.

But the truth remains that many moderate sized communities around the country often squeeze unnecessary and illogical levels of public transportation into the budget each year. It's often a utopian effort at modeling a community after an ideal that is attractive to a very select group of people. It goes mostly unnoticed however because many citizens do not realize the cost that is allocated for over- issuing public transportation. Busses with many empty seats means that it can be scaled back; the convenience of public transportation can cost time but shouldn't waste money.

What's Right?

Drawing from history, public transportation, like many other public entities, is what Thomas Paine might take the occasion to call a "right-wrong." Or perhaps he'd call it a "wrong-right?" Either way, one of his theories, taken from his book "Common Sense," was that sometimes things become so commonplace in society, so accepted in life, that they seem to be right; though perhaps they may be developed under a wrong set of ideals. In today's America, there isn't a person alive who would recall the days when there was no public transportation available, so it tends to feel "right." In fact, there are conceivably many persons who believe that the government is somehow obligated to provide it.

I am not making the case that all of public transportation is unnecessary and ought to be eliminated. However, I believe, as many other logical people do, that the system exists at levels that are unrealistic and are so because of ideology and not real needs. Public transportation should adhere to pragmatism and operate at a level which is necessary and paid for primarily by its riders. It is operated with a "wrong" notion of the use of public funds. It's wrong to take from others to provide a service for but a few for the purpose of luxury. But the truth is that public transportation has become such a fixture of American society that it has become a "right" in the eyes of many. And I would say that is just plain "wrong." Right?

Public Spending Reduction: Healthcare

The topic of healthcare will be a subtopic of the larger "Public Spending" chapter because the fact is that healthcare is slowly becoming a government responsibility in this country and to be frank…that's not cool. When the government implements programs to aid in the payment of healthcare, it costs a lot of taxpayer money. It's one of the biggest, if not the biggest, expenditure of the federal and local governments and it should be zero, or very close to it. At least that's what logic would dictate.

A citizen's health coverage should be something that is personal and taken care of, financially, the same way any other expense is. That translates to say that a person's healthcare costs should be theirs alone to deal with and not become the responsibility of other people unwillingly. And when the government pays for or partially subsidizes healthcare it is "other people" paying for it. It's true that the price of health coverage is high in some cases but that's not the fault of the healthy people or the "other people." Liberals will make the case for the community as it pertains to healthcare and utilize the government to pay for expenses. But this, again, is taking away the responsibilities that should be the onus of the individual, not to mention it distorts real market pricing in the health industry.

Conservatives generally do not believe that the government is better at facilitating private market industries than are the industries themselves. Nor does government have a good sense of how to fairly regulate them. Healthcare is no exception. If government bureaucrats attempt to "fix" healthcare by way of interjecting policy into the industry, it generally makes it worse. Healthcare gets particularly intervened with because liberal politicians will make it into a humanitarian effort of goodwill. Some may even go so far as to espouse healthcare as a basic human right; akin to such rights as freedom of speech.

But again, that's the way liberal politicians siphon votes; by allowing citizens to believe that they are deserving of something with or without effort put forth to obtain it.

It takes a misinterpretation of rights for one to embrace the notion that healthcare is a right. No human has the right to have their healthcare provided to them. They do, however, have the right to obtain it if they choose to, but they do not have the right have it regardless of circumstances; rights do not work that way. Liberals will often make the case that it is indeed a right but that is an argument that is based purely on emotion and, to some degree, entitlement. This argument is used as a way to make those who would interpret rights as privileges of freewill into naysayers of peoples well being. This is because conservatives do not believe that anyone is entitled to the services of healthcare anymore than they are entitled to the services of a manicurist.

Regardless of rights, government cannot effectively run or oversee a healthcare program because it requires a lot of infrastructure, people, and time; not to mention that it is not the role of the government to facilitate. Citizens have always had to be responsible for their own well-being and body's health. Only recently has the idea of "government healthcare" become what it has. Unfortunately, the average citizen is unaware of the enormous pressure and expense this puts on a government which is not equipped to manage healthcare. The functions of the government were never intended to pay for medical coverage, even for the frail or elderly. Perhaps some cost assistance can be had, but even at that it begins a precedent which can and has grown exponentially.

People should be aware that the longevity of their lives is their responsibility and as a species it is prudent to take measures at self-preservation. This can be done in many ways, such as: obtaining health insurance, saving money specifically for health needs and/or eventually living close to family for needs. Despite the high cost of some healthcare procedures, citizens need to take responsibility for it because when it's government that pays the cost, it's actually other taxpayers who pay the cost. And most people do not want to pay for other's healthcare. Government should not provide funded, free or subsidized healthcare to anyone who is more than capable of doing for themselves.

Some detractors of the notion that healthcare is a personal responsibility will compare it with the "right to an attorney" Miranda reading that accompanies arrest. But that is different for this reason: the judicial system is riddled with procedure, and when a person is incarcerated they may or may not have the ability to understand the procedure, and/or have the mental or emotional stability to conduct a legal defense, depending upon what the crime entails. Thus one has the "right" to be represented (usually by a lawyer) so society can ensure that every attempt is made to get the verdict correct. Jailing innocent people is not good precedent. This is in direct relation to the Fifth and Sixth Amendments (Bill of Rights) which were written to ensure fairness in a time when royalty ruled and justice was unfair and brutal.

This particular "right to an attorney" is more of a check on government to hold the judicial system to account than it is a real right. An example might be this: a person loses a loved one to murder and they may not have the emotional capacity to both grieve and perhaps prove their innocence if they are in fact a suspect. The person can have a law professional help them with legal proceedings, ensuring they are treated fairly by those who must oversee that justice be made right. That's logical. But healthcare is a decision that can be made long before anything dramatic happens to a person, so it's up to the individual, not the government, to make sure they are able to pay for their medical costs.

There are laws in the United States that prohibit emergency-care providers from refusing to treat a person who comes into their facility even if they suspect that the person cannot pay for the care they will receive. I suppose that on the surface that seems reasonable considering most situations which bring people to emergency rooms are crises and life-saving procedures. But perhaps there ought to be an ensuing law which makes failure to pay for emergency services a wage garnishing offense, the way tax evasion would be. This does not remove the ability for care to be administered, but it would help to keep health coverage a personal responsibility; not to mention discouraging non-emergency visits from hypochondriacs and "free loaders."

Healthcare: The Richest Country in the World

There is a purposely misconstrued argument that liberals like to use in an effort to make healthcare a problem only solvable by government. The statement generally goes something like: "We live in the richest country in the world and yet we have so many people unable to get health coverage." And if that statement is made with any level of belief, then the ignorance that is portrayed by a statement like that is frustratingly bothersome. Liberal politicians will generally use that logic in an effort to mislead voters with false emotion. It's sad to know that some constituents will attempt to regurgitate the argument. What's missing in the equation is real logic. The United States medical services have become the "best" in the world because of who the American people are, not the other way around. The level of medical technology is a result of the kind of efforts people put forth in a free-market driven economy.

The United States did not become the "richest" country in the world because it handed out services to people who couldn't afford them or chose not to budget for them. Likewise, this country did not become the success that it is while simultaneously enforcing the notion that citizens have a right to services that they clearly do not. America became the amazing country that it is because it is derived from people who were and still are willing to leave their homes and start anew in a far-off land. The success can also be attributed to the fact that a system of governance has been developed which holds citizens accountable for themselves and adheres to a free-market system.

The framers of the "system" decided it was best to let people rely on themselves. There were no dictatorships, monarchs, or oligarchs. A country can become great when the power of the individual is unleashed and people rely on themselves rather than being coaxed or scared into relying on a central, powerful government. Self-reliance and independence are the precise reasons why conservatives do not like the government taking control of or subsidizing any industry or entity that it really has no business being involved in. When individuals rely on themselves, in a market with other individuals doing the same, it is the best defense against corruption. Everything in life can be corrupted and when it's government that is in control, that corruption is terribly hard to avoid.

Healthcare: The Cost

Allow me to say that I'm proud of the fact that America has become such a medically advanced country. The best doctors and institutions reside in America and there is no denying that fact. But what tends to really bother conservatives is that some people on the left try to turn this amazing profession and the wonderful advances it's made into yet another government mandated entitlement. Government regulation and bureaucratic red-tape is not what's made it so successful; hard work on the part of doctors and tech companies has.

It is not a right but a privilege to live in a country in which doctors and others have worked so hard to bring about the best in medical care. Nobody has a right to their services anymore than they do the right to a plumber, accountant or chimney sweep. Logic should dictate that fact despite the emotion of the issue. Medical advancements can certainly improve and save lives but the means to obtaining it is still a personal responsibility. The mode of thinking by some that healthcare is a "right" bequeathed simply by being alive has played a role in ballooning the costs.

People should have a good sense of what it takes to lead a generally healthy lifestyle, and if they don't, then they're part of the problem. A person's health and well being starts long before they are in need of any real care. Unfortunately, there are many people leading very sedentary and unhealthy lives and they tend to need care, or are told they do, more often. Thus, even if one has health insurance that they provide, it gets used more often than it's intended which forces more services to be rendered and prices to go up. But when it's government paying for it the responsibility factor is taken almost completely out of the equation and there is no incentive to budget via deductibles or co-pays.

In that type of model, there is no incentive for patient or doctor to exercise frugality; and even in healthcare people can be cost effective. A government-paid-for model of healthcare tends to bring people into the doctor's office for the most minor of ailments simply because they can and they're not paying for it. So the more people that are going to the doctor, the less time a doctor has per patient, and hence the more tests and medicine gets offered out in an attempt to accommodate. People need to take care of themselves, make healthy choices and be logical about healthcare. It's really that simple.

Public Spending Reduction: Public Service Announcements/Aid

Most people have heard the commercials on the radio or television that advertise public health and services for things like problem gambling, smoking, parenting and so on. They tend to sound very helpful and caring and are usually accessed via a website or phone line. But these are simply more government created entities that spend money on services that the government should probably not be offering.

People need to ask themselves if it is really necessary for the government to spend millions of dollars to inform citizens that smoking is bad for them. Or worse, to create whole bureaucratic departments with the intention of instructing people how to be a good parent. Admittedly it's a nice message and could possibly offer some needed advice for some but most likely they're not as successful as to justify the amount of money spent.

Again, despite being a good message to send the question is whether it's a necessity or even appropriate for the government to spend taxpayer money this way. Perhaps it's not one of the largest expenditures for government, nonetheless, do citizens really want taxpayer money spent on websites or bureaucracies or other do-good information? That proposition seems endless as there are many people in this country with many problems. If the government offers help for addictions to gambling then they would seemingly have to extend that help to every type of addictive behavior; and that would be expensive.

There are some well-meaning messages and services in the way of websites, bureaucracies and other government-run organizations but the logical conclusion is that they are not necessary. The government can still be a good and moral entity without spending money to promote public health. There are many private and religious-based organizations that already voluntarily provide this kind of assistance. The government can help the cause by doing what it does now: loosening the tax burden for private organizations that provide aid and services. The government does not, however, need to double down and direct taxpayer funds into developing websites and agencies.

As a conservative rooted in logic, I'm not implying that people won't screw up and thus people in need be damned. I'm simply making the point that many of the public service messages and agencies are directed toward those whose problems can generally be interpreted as self-inflicted. If people are in desperate need of help from addiction or hard situations, the government should not be the place they seek help. Government assistance should be a last resort. However, by promoting such services over the airwaves, it's my belief that people with problems are being offered an endless cycle of fouling up and then receiving unbiased help. The truth is that the help some people need should be incentivized; otherwise that help is a band-aid and not a life changer. And if someone really needs government advice on how to be a parent…my advice: don't have children.

Public Spending Reduction: Everything

The U.S. government spends enormous amounts of money without much regard to accountability or responsibility. The bureaucracies I mentioned are but a few of the ways the government can and should curb spending. Unfortunately this chapter would dwarf the rest of the book by comparison if I were to list and research all of the ways the government wastes money. The real problem is that elected officials are always able to find constituents or pet projects that require more money. Until we have a majority of politicians in office who value and appreciate the money which is collected from citizens, the spending will continue to increase. Sadly, it doesn't have to.

Every aspect of government spending has cuts that can be made. Education, free school meals, public employee retirement, unemployment benefits, welfare, parks and recreation, fish and wildlife, defense-the list goes on. Some of these cuts need to be large and some can be small, but the government-the people-need politicians with the courage to produce these cuts in spending. Conservative politicians like the idea of the government being as fiscally responsible as possible and making decisions based upon the logical needs of a community. In other words, they don't like wasting money. And that's a pretty cool attribute.

Chapter 8
Gay Rights

This chapter will be entitled "Gay Rights" though the designation is a political misnomer perpetrated by liberals to make it seem as though gay persons are somehow denied specific rights; thus by supporting "gay rights" they can appear noble. The chapter will not be long because, as a conservative and logical thinking person, the idea of this as a political issue is nonsense. However, due to the fact that the liberal media wants to make it of utmost importance so they can, as well, be perceived as noble warriors, I feel compelled to write about it.

The government is not in the behavior business, nor should it be. As I mentioned, the issue of gay rights is really a façade that liberals use to give conservatives the appearance of being against certain other people. Conservatives have not the slightest problem with homosexual persons. To think otherwise is to have been brainwashed. The issue of gay rights primarily stems from laws that recognize only heterosexual marriages as legal by the state. This has been the case for a long time in most states because, for better or worse, the issue of homosexuality was mostly taboo. In recent years we've come to understand it better as a community and people are no longer ostracized because of it. And that is a good thing.

As a logical thinking person I'd have to agree, however, that when it comes to familial make-up, I do believe that the model of father, mother and children is the best for the children. It's not the only model, but in a loving relationship, it's best for the children to have the influence of both a mother and father. Genders matter insomuch as they guide most people's natural inclinations. Thus, for a boy to have a father figure and a mother figure, it helps solidify the masculine tendencies and feminine respect that boys would naturally want to gravitate toward into adulthood. To argue that a two-father family is the equal to a father-mother relationship is to depreciate the role of motherhood…and vice-versa.

Gay folks who think that conservatives are out to rid society of homosexuality are unfortunately badly misinformed. Or perhaps they're looking for ways to become victims. Either way, they ought to realize that conservatives do not seek to disqualify gay families. In fact, if it brings stability to the children in a home, then the gender balance is only one part of the equation. However, when it comes to what should be legally recognized, there is gray area that will inevitably rise up when American society chooses to change the definition of marriage.

For gay partners, there are legal definitions that apply when they are together and want to be given the same privileges that come with marriage (taxes, hospital visitation, etc…). Whether it's a "domestic partnership" or whatever other name it may be given, no real conservative would argue that this kind of equality should not extend to gay partners or anybody who wants their relationship to be legally recognized but not designated a marriage. But the legal definition of marriage will be skewed into legally recognizing things like multiple partners and other less common types of living agreements if it is changed. Again, people can choose to be who they want, but when it involves children, society should seek to ensure that there is a "best" model.

Changing the definition of marriage does nothing to give any more rights to anyone; but some people think that championing this change is somehow showing conservatives up. They believe conservatives have an anti-gay agenda and this is a direct repudiation of what liberals think is somehow an unequal distribution of rights. Well, as for myself and many other conservatives, let me say that they've won nothing. There have been no rights gained by "legalizing" gay marriage because there was never any absence of rights. Legal recognition of a relationship is not a right. Sure, public opinion about social acceptance is changing; and I believe that should be a positive. Nobody deserves to be stigmatized for who they are. But working to change the legal definition of marriage will have trickle down consequences that, though unintended, will begin to reshape the familial lifestyle in America. And that can't be a good thing for the children.

Some may argue that gay marriage does not change the definition because the definition is "two people." But that's obviously a red herring because the definition is in fact one man and one woman. To reiterate, however, conservatives do not believe that this somehow excludes gay partners from having families. The real percentage of gay persons is small but they are not disregarded because of that. It's true that some see it strictly as an "act" and not the "who" but rather the "what" some people are. Any logical thinking person knows that being homosexual is not an act. But changing the definition of marriage opens the door, not only to other situations such as multiple partner relationships becoming legally recognized, but for others to act their way into the role of marriage to become the next contrarian.

Chapter 9
Guns

It used to seem somewhat baffling to me that the issue of guns and the right to ownership was a modern day political issue. For the right to own is clearly laid out in the Bill Of Rights. However, when one understands the liberal position and mind-set, which looks to alleviate responsibility and shift it away from the individual, the answer as to *why* becomes obvious. The modern media and its coverage of the use of guns against innocent people by persons with killer motives have fueled many citizens to look to the government for solutions to these mindless tragedies. But government cannot give answers or solutions, it can only legislate and regulate. And in this case, legislation and regulation means that good people lose rights because of bad people.

The reality is that gun violence against the innocent is not a new concept. And no matter how much some liberals wish to create a gun-less utopia, it's impossible. In a nation of hundreds of millions, the rate at which guns injure or kill is remarkably low. However, when it is covered on the front pages of newspapers and on the cable news networks every time a gun is used in a horrific fashion, it gives the appearance that it happens much more than it does. And for liberal politicians who want to ensure that it is they who appear to be the safeguards of society, that perception is just fine. The more it appears to be a problem that they can solve with their political power, the more it benefits them.

The real problem is that many liberals and those who want to severely restrict gun use, view guns as nothing more than a tool made for killing. The desire to kill, however, is not what most gun owners harbor inside their beings. A firearm is a recreational tool as well as an excellent provider of protection. When used properly, they pose no imminent threat of death. It may come as a shock to many liberals and gun-abolishment persons, but most gun owners do not want to die. Thus when a firearm is purchased by a responsible person, the protocol for safety is taken very seriously.

That's not to say that owning a gun does not have risks. And it is perfectly logical to be required to register a firearm with authorities. But too often the risk of the gun being used as a weapon against innocent people blinds some on the left from ever seeing a firearm as anything more than a killing machine. Again, liberal politicians will act upon these fears and use false logic to assume the role of the do-gooder. Their motivation is transparent when we understand their desire to be viewed as heroic legislators of the people.

Emotional people will overhype the negative possibilities that a gun brings with it and the politicians will use selective promotion to further the perception of guns as inherently bad.

Responsible people can and do own and carry firearms and don't murder people or allow them to be compromised. There is indisputable data (of which I will not impress upon the reader) that concludes that in fact in areas where there are more responsible people owning guns, coupled with less restrictive gun regulation, the incidents of gun violence is very low. I suspect it is because those who want to use guns against the innocent are actually cowards and the thought of being fought back against is much less sensational.

The gun equals control to those cowardly enough to terrorize innocent people; but a second gun balances the fight and the control is taken away. This is why many of the incidents of random gun violence end in suicide. The coward not only can control the fear he or she instills in the innocent, but they get to opt out at their own discretion. Dying from a bullet shot from another gun means they ultimately lost the battle; whereas with suicide the perpetrator feels like they've won…until (insert version of Hell).

The Second Amendment

The Second Amendment in the Constitution (Bill of Rights) indeed does inform us of our right to keep and bear arms. It justifies the right to bear arms by stating that citizens must be able to form a "militia" for self defense, presumably from the federal government should it ever flex its military muscles toward any or all of the states. Admittedly it does sound like a far-fetched scenario by today's standards, but this was written at a time when that possibility was modeled around the world. Not to mention that most historically successful societies were up-ended because those in power became too powerful and imploded. Conservatives generally understand that this amendment was written in a different time but the idea of self defense is what is most important.

Excitable, liberal people often make reference to the right to bear arms and mock conservatives because of the language. Conservatives know that the justification of the Second Amendment has developed into liberal taunts about "assault" weapons and hunting deer. The Second Amendment is not about hunting deer, it's about self defense. Americans have a duty to protect themselves against harm. Whether that harm comes from an overreaching, aggressive government or a stranger in the neighborhood, a gun is the best form of protection. And guns that shoot a lot of bullets very fast are better defense than those that shoot a single shot. Though the authors of the Constitution probably couldn't have envisioned the type of weaponry available in the 21st Century, the importance of self defense is how the Second Amendment ought to be interpreted.

Murderous Rampages

Undoubtedly, most Americans have seen or heard the results of crazy people taking guns into schools or malls and shooting innocent people to death. It's an egregious act done by, like I mentioned previously, cowardly and sick individuals. Statistically, based on logical observation, it's plain to see that a certain small percentage of people in this world are cowardly and sick enough to commit these grisly murders. Unfortunately, normal people must share their world with crazy murderers and there's not much that can change that. Of course as the world and America move further away from values and religion and closer to personal, feel-good agendas, the result will inevitably empower the insane to shed what small amount of dignity they may have; which may have otherwise stopped them at their thoughts.

The argument from persons on the left is that guns give these lunatics an easy method by which to carry out their cowardly bloodlust. Admittedly, the firearm does make it easy for the insane person to inflict a lot of pain very quickly. But that does not make it the fault of the firearm. It is simply the vehicle the crazy person used to carry out their evilness. The fact that the gun can turn a murderous rampage from one or maybe two victims by some other means, into eight or nine with a gun is why there is so much political attention given. But even a single innocent person dying at the hands of a cowardly-crazy person is just as tragic.

Liberalism turns to government often because to them a government solution is the easiest answer. Legislating or creating new regulations is often seen as a small, if not symbolic, measure against something that has been deemed unacceptable. However, the only thing that is truly accomplished by knee-jerk legislation in response to gun violence is allowing the next restriction on whatever to be easier. Short of making most firearms illegal and forcibly confiscating private property, there isn't any legislation that can put an end to random gun violence. Americans understand that freedom from government intervention is worth risking certain things; lest the next restriction limit something someone else enjoys.

Checking Emotions at the Door

In America in the 21st Century, there is a growing notion that guns equal power. It's not just the insane and cowardly person who equates guns to power, but careful observation would note that guns are becoming a status symbol even among suburban dads. Of course, there is a stark difference in ownership and showmanship versus using a firearm to kill innocent people. Nonetheless, this machismo, if I may call it, is no doubt the product of a few industries touting the glorification of guns and the apparent bravado that comes with owning a powerful weapon. In many movies and in many video games of the modern era, the gun is used to kill and maim and there is no emotion attached to it. It's done simply as an act or play and the violence of the scenes becomes a mere byproduct.

The reader here need not worry though. I will not interject a diatribe which seeks to blame the violence on the big screen for what will happen in the real world. Though many people are certainly influenced by what they see on television, violent or otherwise, it should not be blamed for actions thereof. Video games and movies, when played or watched in context, are not inherently dangerous; much the same way that firearms are not. The right context, however, is not always taught and some very impressionable minds will be subject to the violence without genuine oversight or due diligence to what it means. Parents and responsible adults need to instill this context in children at a young age if they choose to allow them to view such things.

There is a certain irony that radiates from the media and Hollywood however. Often it is those who can command a large audience by means of their popularity who inundate the public with messages supporting restrictive gun legislation. In other words, many actors and musicians and media types will use their pulpit to campaign for restricting that which is so prevalent in their industry: the glorification of guns. As a conservative, rooted in logic, I understand that this glorification is not the ultimate cause, but many of these industry liberals do not afford that same logic to gun ownership. Logical people understand it's not movies, news coverage, song lyrics or video games that ultimately cause people to murder and it's not guns that are the cause. The cause is evil, and society will have a hard time prying that out of existence.

But gun violence is an emotional issue and conservatives understand this. We are not somehow immune to the potential destruction that guns can cause. Crazy people don't ask whether one is pro-gun or not before they open fire in a crowded place. Gun violence, to be quite frank, sucks and I wish it could stop. It changes lives forever and the truth is it probably does happen more often than it should. Logic would dictate, however, that society can enact the most restrictive gun policies, lengthen the "waiting periods" one must go through now or attempt to outlaw guns altogether and evil will still find a way. These measures only really affect the good people that want to own guns for recreation or protection. Overbearing rules against firearms will never stop them from getting into the hands of the cowardly and crazy. Rules don't apply to crazy.

As normal people, most citizens have a hard time understanding the thought process of a crazy person and the desire to murder the innocent. I would say that it's safe to conclude that as American society slips further away from religion this type of violence has increased. Myself, I won't lament about religion as I'm not one to talk…but the need for liberal politicians to continue to secularize society might help to explain why people more and more devalue life. Most religions espouse the benefits of family, honesty and servitude; none of which should lead to violence. Mental illness is only one part of the equation as it pertains to crazy. If religion brings nothing else, it brings consequence. But it does, despite liberal hatred for the moral aspect, help people to understand the value and specialness of all life.

Perhaps allowing responsible people to have and carry guns might actually be better for society today. To what extent they can, they might curb evil or at least help to combat it. Government can work to limit certain types of firearms but that really only ends up hurting the good people more. Society doesn't need bazookas or rocket launchers to be sold retail, but it does not need government officials trying to equate semi-automatic guns with the root of the problem. No matter how few guns, big guns or automatic guns there may be in society, there will always be crazy people who cannot control their rage. Again, even if the United Stated Federal Government criminalized mere ownership of guns, they will never disappear.

On their own, guns are not inherently dangerous and allowing emotion to cast blame on them is not responsible. I am not a gun owner, but I know many responsible people who are and have never, and will never, have an incident of intentional human violence involving them. Thus, society cannot simply take these products away from them anymore than they can take the Corvette away from the sports car lover. For one could argue that sports cars are more dangerous than other cars because of their ability to perform at high rates of speed and quick acceleration. There are rules to be followed both on the road and with guns, and when they are, there is no imminent threat of harm. Where America is now in terms of how people relate to each other, there is probably no real or easy solution to ending crazy murderous rampages.

In concluding it must be noted that society doesn't

cast this type of blame elsewhere. For instance there is no blame on food for obesity; the blame is on the individual consumer of food, despite the availability of it 24 hours a day. There is no blame on legal gambling for squandered paychecks; despite the allure of winning millions. Thus it's safe to say society should check its emotions, and not its guns, at the door. The easy thing to do is to blame gun violence on the guns; the right thing to do is to blame the gun users.

Chapter 10
Global Warming

In the modern arena of politics, the issue of carbon output is a "hot" topic. The term "Global Warming" became a buzz phrase sometime in the early to mid 1990s. Oddly, if this book were being written in the 1970s, this chapter might be entitled "Global Cooling." In modern politics, the left is convinced that carbon output is melting the planet, whereas in the 70s they were convinced that a coming ice age was upon them. The topic of global warming and carbon output is a great example of how liberal politicians create or exacerbate emotionally-charged, doomsday scenarios in an effort to make themselves appear selfless or magnanimous; all the while they're berating citizens who dare question their motives or the science behind the theory.

The science behind the theory is roughly this: pockets of air trapped underground have high levels of carbon…those pockets were from many, many years ago when the Earth may have been warmer…

thus carbon output by man-made machinery will eventually add too much carbon and warm the Earth back up. This assumption is based on the greenhouse gas effect that CO2 has as it keeps heat trapped in the atmosphere. But the science isn't really scientific as much as it is an assumption or a model of what more carbon might mean. There is no actual proof that more CO2 will warm the globe. But they don't say that…because scientists need federal grants for research and politicians need constituents to be afraid of something (something they can fix).

Many people, politicians included, get hung up on the belief that 90-some percent of "scientists" believe global warming to be true, thus it must. But how big is this sample of "scientists" and is it possible when asked about the probability versus the model, they may have a different opinion? The supposed temperature increases that have been measured, which amount to about half a degree, have historically been measured at ground level and in less than variable free zones. This should make obvious the fact that these measurements could be wrong or unreliable at best. Thus, there is skepticism about the sensationalizing of an imminent threat.

That doesn't stop the liberal politician, however, from latching onto the notion of a doomsday scenario to further their appearance of the "do-gooder." They have an ever-present need to constantly feel like they're making citizen's lives safer, when in fact they're just making it more rule-oriented. Rules, while necessary when logical, restrict freedom. Casting rules and regulations about, without truly understanding the issue makes for very vague comprehension as well as reluctant adherence on the part of those who become affected.

To be clear, conservatives are skeptical that global warming is a threat but that doesn't mean there is somehow a disregard on our part about environmental responsibility. Are there some parallels in the science?....Yes. But that doesn't make it scientifically proven. There are more and more "scientists" coming out everyday who admit that the rise in CO2 (parts per million) may not actually work to raise the temperatures. As well, they admit to not being certain whether the high carbon levels measured in dirt pockets were the cause or effect of a warm globe.

Science is a fact or fiction field of study and not a speculative one. Thus, if there is doubt then there's no conclusiveness. Besides, is it not fair to ask whether the models are a true indicator of a coming threat? Likewise, could not a logical person ask whether the pockets of trapped air which are measured have been naturally manipulated over time due to the fact that they are indeed…underground? The Earth, by most "scientific" measures, is a pretty resilient thing. Conservatives tend to understand this and generally have more faith in both humanity and the rock they reside on.

Apocalypse (if not now) When?

Liberal people are, as we've discussed, more emotional, more excitable types of people. Thus, to an emotionally excitable person the thought of living in the generation of people facing the "end of times," on Earth, must seem…exciting. It's a timeless proposition, really. All throughout history it's easy to see that there have been many societies with many beliefs regarding the end of the Earth. Often the end of the Earth is prophesized and thought to be close or imminent. Natural disasters, war, and disease could have lent credence to ancestral beliefs that the end of the world was in fact near. And in some extreme cases, it may have truly felt like the Apocalypse to some generations.

The generation before mine was plagued with the fear of nuclear warfare amongst the United States and the USSR. It was thought to be virtually inevitable and it would bring about the world's destruction. Then that generation grew up and had children and they realized that it wasn't inevitable; the world did not blow up. But having something of importance to fear and politicize is what liberal politicians feed on.

Today's emotional-class is no different. They need something to fill that void of generational importance. Disease, war, terrorism and natural disasters occur but they don't feel like they are an imminent threat to destroy the Earth. But high levels of carbon output, produced by a greedy and technological world of humans no less, fills that void nicely. When the pockets of air were measured this side of the Industrial Revolution, the emotional and alarmist crowd were on to something big. They had a cause for this generation to latch on to; and to boot, it could be blamed mostly on "big industry." Something that liberals are told they must verbally defile.

Industry is a word that has come to be synonymous with greed as the byproducts of industry have become an easy target for liberal thinkers; which includes many in the scientific community. Many of these liberal thinkers already take issue with industrialism based upon their inherent distrust of capitalism; because industry means capital. Thus, global warming made for a two-fold argument which could be both this generation's doomsday scenario as well as a way to politically demonize human industrial behavior. It becomes a warm straw-man in a way; build up the phenomenon so as to crush industrialism.

This conclusion by "scientists" that human industrial behavior has raised the level of carbon in the atmosphere and warm temperatures will be the result is purely speculative at this point. The conclusion is pre-based upon the pockets of air. But when one thinks about this argument logically it's easy to understand how liberal politicians can be so manipulative. To some, it feels just to create an image of destructive human behavior, if only so one can curb their own behavior slightly; just enough to feel like they're not part of the problem…as much.

Human societies have seemed to enjoy or embrace this notion of living in apocalyptic times for this reason: it applies an importance to their time on Earth. Perhaps it's because liberal secularists feel as though their time on Earth is a revolving door of galactic human existence. It would be pretty gloomy to think that one's time on Earth is all they have. Global Warming applies an importance to this Earthly existence that could in fact breed hysteria if it appears threatened. The issue of global warming gives liberals, exploitative liberal politicians, liberal scientists, liberal news anchors and the hippie down the street reason to be frenzied and administer importance to their generation's time on Earth. I suppose that's what they think they need to do to be cool (pun).

Preservation Consternation

Another big misconception that the *everyday liberal* has about the *everyday conservative* is that we don't value the cause of environmental preservation and as a result we rarely recycle or take part in small efforts of conserving. Though it's true that many conservatives are skeptical of the imminent threat posed by carbon emissions, that skepticism does not mean that we don't see the value to having a clean place in which to live. We, unlike our counterparts, believe that humans need to be reasonable in the approach to dealing with issues of environmental concern. Too often the approach is knee-jerk and scenarios arise where unnecessary regulation or concern leads to the unnecessary disruption of human development. Needless over-regulation leads to people having to needlessly adjust otherwise normal commerce practices or lifestyles. It's as though some extreme environmentalists forget that humans are part of the ecosystem too.

The truth is that most conservatives don't look at human innovation as a bad thing. As logical, thinking beings we have the capability of conservation and environmental friendliness in that which we produce. In other words, humans ought to strive to create cleaner burning machines, develop more ways to recycle and keep waste to a minimum. But we don't need to go overboard in the rhetoric about situations which need further scrutiny. We don't need a separate industry whose focus is on the doom scenario of polar ice melting and penguins and polar bears floating away on tiny icebergs.

Logic should dictate to most: it seems far-fetched that human industry, in the relatively few industrial cities on Earth, could change the weather patterns of the world. I'm not sure one has to be a "scientist" to come to that conclusion. Not to mention that "scientists" have been wrong with previous conclusions which have come to be seen as "no-brainer's." For instance, it wasn't all that long ago that science and medicine did not believe cigarettes to be necessarily harmful or toxic to the body. And scientists in the 1970's thought the Earth was going through an ice age. The illusion that scientists are donned in white coats and do nothing but study science allows for some to believe that everything "scientific" must be true. But agendas exist everywhere in society; even in science.

Conservatives do not discount entirely the effects of carbon output on the Earth's atmosphere. As a result they're not coming up with slogans advocating for "brown lifestyles" to offset the "green agenda" of most environmentalists. Instead, conservatives are reasonably skeptical that the Earth is under assault by burning fossil fuels. We generally agree that improving the efficiency of such burning is ultimately a good thing. However, hysteria about carbon and a theory that says more of it means more heat is not something we'll believe just because. The reason is simple: the data is not there to support it and it's plain to see the model data has since been manipulated.

I have faith that humans recognize when change is necessary and then....we change what needs changing. The majority of people will get milk, for instance, before the last gallon runs out at home. I like to think that humans are collectively like that as well. Thus, we won't be killing ourselves off in an artificial heat wave and we won't let the Earth's milk supply run out either.

Weather or Not It's Related

There is a political calculation going on as it pertains to the theory of global warming perpetrated by those who need to believe it to be true. With the emphasis on global warming and the hyper-excitement being stirred up in response, in today's society almost every weather-related incident is being blamed on "climate change." If one is savvy then they caught the change in classification from global warming to climate change. The fact is that this anxiety was originally classified as global warming because conventional wisdom was that human carbon output would warm the globe.

But the temperatures aren't rising and the massive destruction that was predicted 15-20 years ago has not happened either. Thus, the new name of "climate change" has been adopted because the liberal, excitable people still need a disaster scenario to apply importance to their generation. This includes so-called "scientists" whose predictions were initially wrong and who now need a back-up theory in an attempt to still be "scientifically," possibly correct. In essence what they're saying is that human activity may not warm the globe, but it will in fact cause drastic and inclement weather patterns worldwide. In other words…a back-up theory.

What this translates to is every hurricane, tropical depression, heat wave, cold spell and even earthquakes are being blamed on climate change. Of course, it's not as though these incidents never happened before, but the "warmists" will say that they are happening with more frequency. However, it's plain to see that when someone applies "climate change" repercussions to every incident of less than perfect weather, it may seem to them as though something catastrophic is happening.

The reality is that bad weather, hurricanes and tornados and such, do not happen with any more or less frequency than they always have. But if one is led to believe the theory to be true, then they will indeed blame human induced climate change for just about any lousy weather. To illustrate with an example: if someone owed money to a loan shark and was late paying it back, they may believe there to be a recent uptick in traffic on their street. Of course that paranoia would be fueled by the desire to preserve their kneecaps. Can we understand the correlation?

Global Regulation

There are some very prominent persons in this world who would like the theory of global warming to be true so they can actively create government regulations that will help ease the human "carbon footprint." And more regulation means more rules. And more rules means less freedom. And less freedom is… not cool. One can just imagine the over-regulatory ideas liberal politicians could come up with to make themselves feel better about other people's lives and "carbon footprints."

Even if we accept the premise that the globe is warming and humans are the direct cause of it, shouldn't we expect a more rational approach to solving the problem from politicians? It doesn't seem to make much sense to act hysterical and predict gloom. All that does is whip constituents into a frenzy over the issue because many of them are longing for that doomsday scenario in their lives. It causes unnecessary panic.

The other side of that coin is this: if it were truly imminent and the world is already seeing the precursors to global destruction in the way of melting ice, then would it not make sense that government begin the complete retraction of all things that burn fossil fuels? If the climate is already being affected, then it would seem logical that a ban on cars and planes and such should be underway. But the truth is the politicians and "scientists" know it's not really that dire. They simply allow their authoritative agenda to guide their politics…and their science!

Only the Young Die Good

I've talked about liberal people being generally the more emotionally excitable among the population. But when one thinks of people in general, most would probably agree that-political leanings aside-the youth tends to be very emotionally excitable. Young people, let's say ages 18-25, are usually easily swayed by emotional arguments because they do not have a lot of life experience with which to draw conclusions based on comparison. Thus, if certain politicians, highly recognizable celebrities or even the local weather man tells them that the "sky is falling," they just might believe them. They can be duped by good salesmanship much more so than their elders.

Although a majority of young voters usually identify themselves as liberal, not all youth believe the globe is melting. And of course there are many, though thankfully not a majority, of older adults who believe global warming to be true. An interesting question, however, to ask oneself is this: how or why is it that this theory, which is supposedly backed by "science," is generally thought to be true by only certain people? (Certain...more excitable people).

My theory is that liberal politicians know that doom and gloom is a big political seller. Some speculate that it's part of a grand hoax to get funding for science and votes for liberals. Perhaps there is some subconscious truth to that. People can force themselves to believe many things which are untrue. But one thing is certain, doomsday scenarios sell particularly well to the youth; who can blame their predecessors and who still believe that they have time left to do something about it, lest they die young but still good.

As it pertains to the youth vote, global warming is really the "perfect storm." Politicians and other believers can get the youth scared and worked up by utilizing hyperbole and creating movies and documentaries that prophesize the end of the world. Then they will hire them to go door to door in suburban neighborhoods armed with literature that they can barely comprehend in an effort to "get the word out." Thus it creates a solid constituency.

Not to be misunderstood, the politicians and other alarmists would probably like to believe climate change to be factual. My guess is, however, they know it's not so dire. But the youth will believe it and that's a large constituency come voting time. It furthers their agenda to be able to paint naysayers (conservatives) as old, grumpy people destroying the planet with yesterday's technology. I remember my college days and earliest political cognizance. I too was certain that my parent's generation was destroying the planet and it was up to my generation to fix it. At the time…it made perfect sense. But time creates perspective and tends to clear up misguided excitement from our days of youth. Now…I see "climate change" for what it really is: a political weapon.

Chapter 11
Taxes

Taxes and tax collection are the funding source behind many things that make America a great country. The development and use of public roadways, airports, fire and rescue, police and the armed forces are all paid for with taxes collected on the working American public. It's not as glamorous an issue as some political topics but it takes politics to decide who gets taxed and for how much. The method by which most tax is collected is the income tax. The system set up currently is very unsettling and discriminatory. The money itself is often not viewed by politicians the way it should be either. Taxes should and could be a very simple procedure and an equal burden shared by all. I mean…it's just numbers. I don't intend to use too many numbers, as I've said, but with taxes…it's…well, numbers.

There is one important thing to remember as it pertains to "revenue" the government brings in via taxes. That money is earned by the citizens and given to the government in exchange for public services. That money is NOT government money. The government doesn't earn it they take it; which is agreeable if they respect it. Too often, I'd argue, elected officials, and appointed ones as well, show disregard for thrift or accountability when dealing with the spending of tax money. It borders on blatant disregard for the honor that was put into the hard work to earn that money by the citizenry. Reckless accounting and overpaying for projects becomes the norm, while the wasted spending is no more dwelled upon than burnt toast. Government's wasteful spending increases the consistency with which taxes and fees need to be raised.

It's the Economy....

Our country's economic system is based upon the principles of capitalism. It is a term that simply defines the way in which private citizens conduct transactions. Capitalism and a free market economy require a regulatory body, i.e. the government, but it does not require major government involvement into the dealings of the economy. In a capitalist society, money is earned and it's either spent or reinvested. It's free enterprise, which means the ability to conduct business with one's money the way they see fit with a limited government role in the procedure.

This translates, simply, to people competing for other people's dollars; which is what drives people to better their situations. That's why free enterprise in a market economy caters so perfectly to the potential humans have to excel. Often people are at their best when they are competitively pushed by others competing for something they all want.

A large government with high taxation cannot happily coexist with an economy that is meant to grow. The more tax that is levied on businesses and individuals, in an effort to take care of "public services," the less money for the private sector to inject back into itself. Thus, the fewer dollars there are to be competing for. Less reinvestment and spending equates to less growth. Ironically, less growth means lower overall tax revenue to the government. You'd think they'd figure that out.

In terms of tax revenue, there is an easy concept that is hard for liberal folks to ingest and make sense of. The less you tax, the more money the government will ultimately pull in. Lower tax rates stimulate growth, which means people will make more money in the end. And if they make more money, they'll pay more taxes based upon sheer volume. Example: $100,000 income taxed at 35% equals $35,000. What if the rate dropped to 15% over the next five years? That's $20,000 extra dollars per year to the taxpayer. Do you think that extra money might go back into the economy in the form of buying goods and/or starting a business?

People with extra money do "extra" economical things with it. Even if a chunk went to savings and not investment, would that not have a great impact on programs like Social Security and Medicare? People ultimately become more self sufficient when they are able to keep more of their own money. Of course, those who want us to be reliant on their "wisdom" want you thinking otherwise.

Here A Tax, There A Tax....

There are a variety of ways we citizens pay taxes in this country. Over here is an income tax, a sales tax and a property tax...over there is a gas tax, hotel tax, paint tax and licensing fees (which are a tax). Some of us are even taxed when we die. I'm not rich so it won't be me, but some of you!

Many of the elected officials love taxes because they generally don't view it as OUR money. They view their role in government as one of an arbitrator of what shall be. Thus, they believe it's incumbent upon them to spend the money to suit their best interests. If politicians view government as an entity that trumps the people it governs, on matters of finance and otherwise, then they become very self-important. Unfortunately, there is often an accompanying arrogance that prohibits such elected officials from budgeting the public trough with a sense of logic instead of a personal and agenda driven focus. In other words, if they want skateboard lanes, you'll get skateboard lanes.

In the list of taxes above we see the gas tax. Here is an example of a how a tax can be bastardized. The idea behind such a tax is simple. A certain percentage of every gallon of gas sold is taxed with the intent of that money going to the upkeep and maintenance of everything road-related; which probably sounds reasonable to the logical person. We would also probably agree that roads are a necessity and cars that use gas tend to be the primary users of roads. There are multiple levels of government which all tax that gallon of gas from the local up to the federal. That makes sense since different levels of government maintain different roadways systems. That's everything from federal highways to local neighborhood streets.

The taxing is not an issue really. However, the attitude elected officials take is often too controlling as to how the money is to be spent. One would assume that the taxes should be enough to cover expenses, but what if there is a surplus? Leftover money is all too often seen as a pot of gold in which government officials feel it is incumbent upon them to spend. What ends up happening is they use that money for other purposes not pertaining to roads or they'll use it to manufacture road projects that may not be necessary at the time.

A true conservative person or politician would have a desire to hand back any unused or leftover money from any tax or fee that is collected. The problem is that government obligates itself to too much spending and sometimes those obligations don't have a cute, specified tax or fee collection. Thus, they end up borrowing from other funds to make up for the difference. Too much borrowing from Peter to pay Paul will eventually lead Peter to be penny-less and naked. A naked Peter may be ok in some situations but reckless accounting is never too cool.

Progressive Taxation (That's Progress?)

The gas tax is an example of everyone (who drives) paying the same rate of tax for the gas that they purchase, so the roads can be maintained. It doesn't matter if someone drives 100 miles a day or 100 miles a year. Nor does it matter the kind of car; large truck or small soup can sedan. The purchaser is taxed the same rate for each gallon of gas they buy. For example, it may be 10% of the price of the gallon. $3.00 a gallon equals 30 cents tax per gallon. Thus, the more someone drives, creating more wear and tear on the roads, the more they would pay because they're buying more gas. That sounds fair and logical…

However…the income tax structure in this country is not set up so fairly and that should be a major point of contention with everybody. Liberal (emotional) people are very bitter toward high-income earners in this country because they are manipulated to believe rich means evil by the Democratic Party. The manufacturing of bitterness is just a tactic to differentiate classes of people in an effort for Democrat politicians to get votes.

The majority of citizens in this country pay income tax on every dollar they earn. I get that. We need the government to handle certain services that the private sector cannot and should not. As well, those services have to be paid for in some fashion despite the fact that the government does not "earn" money. I can say with relative certainty that there are very few people who would that argue that zero taxation is necessary. It makes sense, as well, for the government to take it directly from each of our paychecks rather than billing people for their tax share. That's easier than running down a bunch of tax evaders.

What does not make sense, however, is that we have established a system of taxing which taxes individual's income relative to how much they make. Translation: The more money a person makes the HIGHER rate of tax they will pay. Imagine if that were true of the afore mentioned gas tax: the more one drives, the higher rate of gas tax they'll pay. It's unfair and it makes no sense. Remember, by applying a percentage rate of tax to the gallon of gasoline, people who drive a lot will be paying more than the people driving less by virtue of the amount of gas purchased.

The question should be asked then, what makes it fair to tax individuals at different rates based upon how much money they make? For example: If two income earners each are charged 5% tax on their income, a person making $100,000 a year pays $5,000 tax while a person making $20,000 annually only pays $1000 in tax. Thus, the higher income earner pays five times the amount of tax than does the lower income earner when paying the same rate. Sorry about those numbers…

It's hard to imagine much rational thought behind the idea of a "progressive" tax rate, which is the concept of taxing people relative to income. Well maybe it's not so hard when you consider the political ammo that it gives Democrats to be able to go after a small constituency like the rich. On the surface, it seems quite un-American.

It's pretty unjust and somewhat sickening to think people are treated differently on a subject matter which constitutes their livelihood. By taxing based upon income, the government is discriminating against families and workers. There really is no rational justification for it other than hyperbole about rich people not paying a "fair share" because they make more money. Fair, to me, would seem to be a level percentage for anyone earning money.

Let's proceed with another anecdote to simplify this a bit. Remember Larry and Cramer? We'll bring them back but this time we'll make them co-workers at an apple picking farm. For the sake of details, we can name the apple farm Mo's Apples. Mo is their boss and we'll say that he has hired both Larry and Cramer to pick apples and has conditionally agreed to pay them based upon the number of apples they pick per day. The more they pick, obviously, the more they are paid.

On day one, let's suppose, Cramer comes out picking like he's on fire. He uses long ladders, bows and arrows and even takes to shaking trees to get the apples. In other words, he picks his ass off. Working virtually non-stop, he picks 1000 apples. Larry, on the other hand, also worked hard but not as efficiently as Cramer. He took the required breaks throughout the day and generally didn't have the zest for apple picking that Cramer did. He comes in at day's end with 250 apples, which is maybe a good day by apple picking standards, but far less than Cramer.

All variables being equal, such as weather and access to bows and arrows, we can conclude that Cramer will get paid more based upon his apple stock.

But let's suppose that Mo, their boss, decided that Larry worked hard but just couldn't keep up with Cramer's enthusiasm for apples and consequently took some apples from Cramer's load to give to Larry. That doesn't seem fair, does it? In fact, we might say "Whoa Mo!"

That is in essence what "progressive" taxation is based upon. The notion that despite hard work, you're not always entitled to everything you earn. This concept actually penalizes people like Cramer for working harder, smarter or for just plain being lucky. It takes away the incentive for Cramer, and other more aggressive earners, to achieve all that they can.

Applying the concept of taxation, let's suppose Mo was obligated to collect an apple tax on the government's behalf. If the apple tax were 5%, then Cramer would need to give up 50 out of 1000 apples and Larry would give up about 12 apples. Just by volume alone, Cramer pays a much greater amount in apple tax than does Larry. That's how our income tax system should and could work if people were taxed at a flat rate for their earnings, regardless of how much money they earn. Yet to change Cramer's percentage to 10% while keeping Larry's at 5% and justifying it based on volume is simply not fair to Cramer. He may as well save the effort.

Policies such as this stifle a person's desire to work hard. It penalizes them for working harder or longer than others. When we micro it down to apples, I think, we're able to envision better how it relates to income tax, which is virtually unseen to most people. But a policy such as progressive taxation represses incentive and it isn't very cool either. In fact, let's just call it un-cool.

Class Warfare (Is Classless)

My objective with this book is to get you (the reader) to think about political issues and politics in general with a sense of logic; hopefully erasing any cloudiness that may exist. The reason: logic is what guides conservative thought and when dealing with an issue like taxes it's no different. What makes logical sense? Ask yourself that question when thinking about the "progressive" tax system we deploy in this country. The philosophy (loosely defined) of taxing people differently…is that a good idea? There is no other tax which we execute with such discrimination. For example if one were to buy a lot of items at the store versus one or two items, they're not charged a higher sales tax percentage.

At a place of business, there may varying levels of management or ownership or co-workers who all make different wages per hour, per year, etc…Is it right for the government to treat them differently? Think of the place you work. Yes you! Would that be right for the government to treat your co-workers differently?

The idea that we need to tax people at different rates is now an engrained philosophy in the minds of some elected officials and constituents. They have their reasons why they think it's good economic policy but it's not based in logic. It's based on emotion. Elected officials know that they have a solid base of voters who are not rich, and they pander to that group with false knowledge about the rich and their intentions. The practice of verbally pitting one group against another, then carrying out economic discrimination via government policy is called class warfare.

The politicians and officials are in office to serve ALL of the people without favorability. Many politicians on the left, and some misguided ones on the right, will use divisive and deceptive language to facilitate a sense of unfairness; knowing that the rich are outnumbered.

If we get to the root of the problem, we'll see that many left leaning politicians exist because they tend to campaign on promises which involve government spending money. Often these financial obligations are to benefit the lower or middle class on the backs of the rich. The country has reached a point, however, in which there is not enough money that can be collected to meet all of the obligations. The debts being accrued on the promise of handouts of other people's money is growing so large that in any given year a tax rate of 100% on all earners wouldn't erase them. Yet we keep hearing of promises from government.

The class warfare heroes continue to beat their warfare drum, telling anyone who will listen, and don't know any better, that the rich don't pay enough. When an honest person crunches the numbers, they will see something entirely different. When we pay attention, they can't fool us like that. I often think government officials are like that friend we have who's always spending money he or she doesn't have. Of course we'll still let that friend buy us a drink at the bar because it doesn't cost us anything. The friend, like the government spenders, must assume the money will just eventually come in, thus they'll continue to make and keep friends who use them for what they have…until they can't; because the money's gone.

This type of class warfare and reckless spending makes me wonder how the Democrat Party finds any constituency or even remotely seems appealing to anyone. I don't understand their tactics because logical people, such as I am, don't think the rich among us are to be looked at differently, hated or taxed out of their minds. Their wealth, regardless of how it was obtained (assuming it was legal) is not a magic pot for the rest of us to dip into.

Part of the routine of bashing the rich is to either espouse or buy into falsehoods about the rich "hiding" their money or somehow not paying enough in tax. It's patently not true. The amount of taxes the rich pay, as a share of the total burden, is far more than what some would have people believe. The breakdown isn't even close to middle or lower class. I promised not to bog this book down with numbers and statistics, so I won't. When it comes to taxes, however, the rich pay the bulk of it; and no truthful argument can be made otherwise.

If our tax system were to change away from a progressive system to a "flat" tax system, the rich would still pay the bulk of the taxes. It would change the culture of discrimination against the rich and allow everyone to pay a fair share. In our progressive tax system, there are millions of people who do not pay any federal taxes. The reason is due to a lower end threshold which excuses tax burdens to those under a certain income level. That doesn't sound fair.

Moreover, who should get to decide where we, as an economy, draw the line in defining who is rich and who's not? The definition is going to be arbitrary at best. If the powers-that-be decide that a family income of $250,000 and above constitutes rich, then it becomes a hard sell to call the family making $245,000 "not rich." We have to decide, as a country, if we really want the government to make that distinction. Collecting taxes at a set rate for everyone seems a more passive and proper role for a government of the people.

Wealth, in this case, is being used as a tool against people. What some making this argument for progressive taxation are missing is the effort that goes into creating wealth. It's not falling off trees. In a majority of the cases of large wealth, the persons earning it may have given up years of their lives devoted to school, trade or entrepreneurship. Often there was a lot of financial sacrifice and tightening of budgets before there was bliss. These earners have families and they have worked hard to secure a great living for them. They are no different than any other taxpayer with the exception of diligence maybe; and diligence should be rewarded, not penalized. Money makes these people easy targets because emotional people will use money as an enemy to garner support.

There are some folks who'll try to make the argument that rich persons and high earning companies utilize and produce more need for certain government services, like waste disposal or large fleets of vehicles, thus creating an argument for higher rates of taxation. But again, one must look at usage vs. percentage. If entities that use public resources do so out of volume of business, then they will no doubt be paying more even when taxed at the same rate. This is not to mention the countless fees local governments assess to private business in lieu of more taxation. Regardless, it's no justification for raising rates on only a few.

This argument gets further muddied when we consider that there are some rich people who often vocalize support for higher taxes via progressive taxation. If we categorically breakdown the demographics of such "Limousine Liberals" we notice that a majority reside in field such as news media, Hollywood and rock n' roll. But their clamoring is transparent. I like to call it the guilt factor.

These folks are talented at their craft, no doubt, however my theory is that a lot of them are thrust very quickly into the limelight with riches and fame, and with that it produces a stigma that this type of work is more a product of good fortune and not talent. This is not necessarily something I believe to be true, in regard to their talent, but deep down there may be resentment from regular people who feel that these fields are populated based more upon vanity than ability. Thus, it translates to many famous people vocalizing liberal talking points despite not really fully understanding the political landscape and/or the real differences between the ideologies. They simply gravitate toward the emotional side to shed some guilt…because they think it's cool.

Corporate Tax

The corporate tax, or "business tax," is the same as the personal income tax, mostly, except it's applied to corporate or business revenue. It taxes based upon sales registered and thus the profit. It's stupid. Why? Any good business owner simply calculates his or her selling price of goods or services based upon the cost to supply those products. One can assuredly say that a tax is but one expense of doing business. Thus, the business man or woman simply applies that cost against the selling price of the goods or services. In the end it's passed on to the consumer via the price tag. Conclusion: Logic would dictate that we ought to do away with the "business tax" and allow the market to set prices based upon market variables. But try telling that to the class warfare crowd; no taxes on Walmart? Their emotions may just make their heads explode.

Taxed to Death

I mentioned it briefly before, but there is a ridiculous tax assessed on people called the estate tax. Its pseudonym is the "death tax" because it taxes a person's wealth upon their death. It generally applies to persons whom have accumulated substantial wealth. There is an amount in which it generally begins at and it's applied to the transfer of the wealth, to persons in the family or not. That's how they make it applicable, by going after it as income to the beneficiaries. In other words, father leaves son an inheritance upon his death; the government says that's an income stream to the son, thus they want some of it via tax. Heartless really…

The tax, to a logical person, is incomprehensible. Yet Democrat politicians, who love to tax the wealthy, will fight long and hard to keep it. This kind of tax is both immoral and technically a double tax. Most of the money that is "transferred" upon death has already been taxed when it was earned. So to tax it again is to double tax it. The immorality is that this money is usually family money earned which would be passed on to other generations of family; to be enjoyed by the earner's family whom are still alive.

The amount that is taxed usually applies to estates whose value rises into the millions, but not far into the millions. Often there's an amount that can be transferred virtually tax free but after that it's taxed at a ridiculous rate of something like 40-50%. The liberals must think they're being generous by "allowing" a certain amount to pass through without penalty, but that's their façade. They make it sound appealing and fair to the majority of persons who do not leave millions of dollars behind by grandstanding about the villainy of the wealthy and doubling down on the class warfare rhetoric.

Almost every conservative politician would tell you that if they could, they would repeal this tax on any level of government; federal or local. If somehow a conservative politician or politicians are in favor of keeping it, then they are really a poor example of a logical thinking person. I would say they need some work on becoming cool. Doing something like this to families because you can and for no other logical reason should be means for their removal from office. It's really a backhanded approach to gain revenue for the government. That's not how elected officials should govern. This tax is patently unfair and does not resemble the attitudes by which this country was founded.

Who Gets to Vote?

Let's start to wind down the tax chapter by addressing taxes that are voted on by the people. We are taxed at the Federal level, as we've discussed, through income tax. We don't vote, per se, on taxes at the federal level other than voting for representatives to Congress. The local level, however, often presents citizens of a county or city with measures asking them to increase fees and/or taxes. These are usually offered in the form of raising rates or one time fees to be collected. In many of the cases the outcome will generally affect everyone who pays taxes or uses whatever government service is being put to vote. However, at times the local officials will ask voters to affect only certain constituents with their vote. In other words, people are asked to raise tax rates on taxes that won't directly affect them.

I'll use two examples of how this procedure affects

certain people by a vote of constituents outside the parameters of the measure. First, there are often measures on the county level which ask voters to raise the property tax rates by X amount. Usually it's a small percentage. In some cases it may be coupled with a justification of raising money to fund schools or construction projects. The problem is that these votes are not cast solely by property owners who will get stuck with the added tax burden. True, some property owners may vote yes to raise rates, however I would argue that only those persons owning property and who will be directly affected should be able to vote on such a proposal.

The left will combat that logic by saying that renters of property are in essence charged the amount to a make up for the tax. This is perhaps true, but not always is that fee able to be assessed immediately due to rental agreements. As well, there are may be thousands of votes cast from persons living in fixed price, government sponsored housing. The argument should be made that only people who will be directly and immediately affected by a tax hike can vote on any measure asking such. That seems pretty logical.

The second example was born from a measure at my own local level several years back. In essence the ballot measure was asking voters to approve a local tax hike on high income earners to settle a gap in funding for teaching positions in the area. Hard to imagine a measure would ask one large group of people to raise the tax burden of a small group of people. But because the liberals can craft vocabulary to ease what most people would see as unjust, we are handed this type of class warfare yet again. Had it been only those high earners who got to vote, then I, nor any other logical person, would have no problem if indeed it were passed. But to present the opportunity for one group of people to sack another with a higher tax is pretty un-American. Even if it were manipulated to sound like a "community" effort, people need to protest this type of classism. If the effort is made to preserve teaching jobs it should be tasked by every tax payer. Asking people to do what you're unwilling to do is not very cool. I mean…really.

Campaign Finance (Donations to Politicians)

In closing the chapter, allow me to touch on a subject that used to be a pretty hot-button issue on the political scene but has lost a bit of fervor over time. It's a money related issue and it can have an effect on tax deductions, hence we'll add it here. Put simply, there was an effort put forth by some politicians to limit the amount of money that can be directly donated to a campaign for a federal position. In other words, they wanted to limit the amount of money they (more importantly their opponents) could receive via donation. The sugar coated argument was that money injected into politics corrupts the political process.

Donating money to a campaign, whether it is from an individual or a corporation, is a matter of freedom and choice. As a conservative, thinking logically, I see nothing wrong with this concept. The persons who want to limit the amount of money to be donated claim those donations, in essence, buy political influence. They argue that high dollar donors will get more access to politicians and may be influential on matters that would benefit the donating party economically or socially. Could that happen? Yes it could. But that shouldn't matter.

Unless the acceptance of donations was a quid-pro-quo for monetary benefit via policy, we citizens ought not to fret. Neither the money nor the donating party is to blame if there are any political deals in return for money. We're not to blame, the politician is. It's not a game of high crimes and big business; it's really something much simpler. I suppose the outcome could result in crimes or big business deals, but again, that's up to the receiving party.

Let's use an example and simplify this. I want to make the case that a politician enacting a rule such as limiting donations, which handcuffs them to the appearance of "doing good," is really sadly ironic. Think of this transaction in a different context. The scenario is a high school biology class. There are students and there is a teacher. If a student wants to give the teacher $100 with the understanding that it will buy him a better grade, the transaction now rests at the feet of the teacher. A good and moral teacher does not accept and in turn gives the student extra homework. However, if the teacher accepts the offer, there's a problem. The student, while perhaps guilty of laziness, is not in the position of authority and thus is simply making a bold attempt at bribery. The teacher has the power and his acceptance of the $100 in exchange for a better grade is what would most negatively affect the situation.

If a politician accepts donations in return for voting or legislative favors then the politician is to blame and not the donating party. The money is really just a bystander and the donating party, though perhaps not an upstanding individual if wanting something in exchange for money, is not the guilty one. The transaction becomes troublesome only if the acceptance is made with the understanding there is something to be done in return for the donation. The politician is the corrupting entity in any attempt to regulate donations. Money doesn't corrupt politics, corrupt politicians do.

Creating legislation to curb or limit campaign finance through donation is a waste of congressional and taxpayer time. It's terribly arrogant on the part of politicians to pass laws limiting citizen donations. That's really as foolish as the husband who blames his wife for his obesity because she enjoys baking cookies. What's not cool is the dishonesty of these politicians as they make the citizenry scapegoats for their own shortcomings. Perhaps a look in the political mirror would better prepare them for the legislative actions of campaign finance reform.

Chapter 12
Poverty

The issue of poverty in America is a political one. Not, however, because of our inherent human desires to take care of our own, but rather it is so due to the process by which we employ vast government resources to do so. There is a multitude of ways in which the government extends financial resources to help people. Countless programs with countless names helping countless groups of people exist all around us. Programs are set up to assist the very needy down to the just slightly lazy. Whether one is the apolitical type or the astute political junkie, they've no doubt heard the endless talking points that abound about mean Republicans and conservatives and how they want to suffocate people who need assistance. That kind of rhetoric is unfortunate and completely false, not to mention just plain old b.s. We could, and I will, argue that conservatives actually care more than their counterparts about the poor. They in fact do so by wanting to offer less, not more, government services.

Live and Let Live

To begin with, the narrative is skewed. Conservatives do, indeed, care about the poor and their well being. However, conservatives also like seeing people make the most of their opportunities in life and succeeding in however they define success for themselves. That attitude makes our society a more livable one. But logic still guides our principles and when one applies logic to the issue of poverty there is but one conclusion: self reliance is the best policy to adhere to.

The liberal politicians like to use poverty as an issue to make themselves and others think that they truly have a vested interest in alleviating the problem. We can decipher this because they talk about the poor is very abstract ways. Their language suggests that they see the poor as a problem they get to throw money at to make it appear as though they're helping. It's as though it's a faceless problem that they'd rather just swoon to ensure a voting bloc. The poor are people not abstractions.

The word "poor" encompasses a variety of levels of income and lifestyle. There are extreme cases of poverty and those just below the poverty line who may be receiving small amounts of government services. But despite the financial situation one finds their self in, the opportunity to get out of it is equal for everyone. Our free enterprise, market economy offers assistance to everyone equally. Some people start higher on the ladder, no doubt, but the opportunity to achieve success does not discriminate.

Capitalism allows us to get out of life what we put into it. I'm going to start this section talking about the upper bracket, if you will, of the poor. Those who have been dubbed: the working poor. Getting out what one puts in does not mean that if one were to work 40 hours a week backfilling ditches they ought to be wealthy based on hard work. That is the part which bothers the emotional class so much. They don't necessarily like that the outcomes people achieve are different, despite the hard work.

A market economy is a system by which people make goods, sell goods and barter goods or services. It places a value on those goods and services based upon the need that exists for them. If there are some people who find great success, it's often due to their working harder, longer or smarter than others. Capitalism rewards those who are able to "capitalize" on the needs of people. Being able to harness wealth by filling people's needs is not greedy because it takes the other party to agree to purchase the goods or services; sometimes in frenzied fashion.

Capitalism allows people to go as far as they want to go in an effort to succeed or do as little as possible to survive. It's a great system for a species with such varying traits and characteristics among us. We're not all the same as we all have different talents, desires, needs, morals, abilities and/or levels of diligence. Some people want to "shoot for the stars," while others are content staying grounded and making do. But some people use that disparity as a way to elevate their political stature.

Unfortunately, the Democrat politician appears to champion efforts of goodwill as it pertains to poverty because they know they can use false emotion to gather support. But the definition of poverty is being skewed and manipulated. We're told it's based on money or resources and how much, or in this case how little, some people have of each. Poverty, however, is not a monetary designation as much as it is a lifestyle; something which exists because people are allowed to be poor. Perhaps that's a strong statement, but follow me as I explain.

Most people who qualify as the working poor are so not because they can't do for themselves, but rather they don't want to do for themselves; or at least just want to do the minimum for themselves. That is by no means a heartless statement. We need to be in tune with the fact that people are allowed to be poor. Their opportunities to heighten their financial situation and lifestyle exist and are no different in terms of filling a market need. In many cases, this type of poverty exists because the people choose a lifestyle with little demand on their time. And that's OK. No one says they can't or shouldn't live that life.

Though this may not be true of every situation in which people are living at or just below the poverty line, I'd argue it's true for most. I have firsthand experience in observing the "working poor". My current employment takes me into people's houses all of the time. I visit the very wealthy down to the "dirt" poor. It's easy for me to see, based on the living conditions of the people I visit, just how little effort some people are willing to put into their own lives. Most cases of poor dwellings are otherwise upright and sturdy structures but it's lack of upkeep which resembles post-apocalyptic conditions.

This observation of mine is not born of a wealthy pretentiousness on my part. I grew up very middle class but with a sense of pride in the home. When I witness truly atrocious living conditions of otherwise healthy and able-bodied people, I'm absolutely bewildered. It comes as no surprise to me that someone accepting filthy living conditions in the home would not be one of society's most successful people.

A lifestyle such as this transcends just the home conditions. It no doubt translates to what type of effort such folks are willing to put in outside the house and into their financial livelihood. Some people are simply unwilling to put in the kind of work and effort necessary to get themselves financially stable and out of poverty. These people can survive, they just won't ever thrive. And it's with these people where we as a society need to begin to cut back on government assistance.

To reiterate, there is nobody and nothing that states that one must work 40 hours a week, keep a clean house and make a certain amount of money. Yet it's hard to logically conclude that some poverty isn't, in essence, a lifestyle choice. Society needs to accept that fact because people are allowed to be what they want to be.

It's not worth accepting the notion that all cases of low-end financial earners need some form of government assistance. If people are able to help themselves but choose not to, that's not a case for assistance. When there are people on food stamps and they are paying for cable t.v, well that's not very cool. It's alright for people to live simply and, like I said before, that's the great thing about capitalism; it allows people to be different…because we are.

Urban Poverty

There could be a case made by some that poverty varies in degree depending upon geography. The argument may be that poverty in small towns, though similar in income levels, is not as large a problem as the generational urban poverty that plagues many metropolitan cities in America. And perhaps, they may say, government assistance is keeping inner city poverty from manifesting a war zone-such that they're not already.

If there is more poverty per capita in metro cities, we need to ask whether decades of government assistance and handing out money has aided the situations or just kept them at a status quo level. I can't claim to be an expert on urban poverty, but I've seen it and it doesn't seem to change much over time. I would make the case that years of government assistance does not force people to make life-changing decisions; it simply keeps them where they are. If in the absence of aid the situations get worse, then as a society we should take appropriate measures such as law enforcement or community driven projects. But to continue to feed the situation of poverty with free money is not an upward trending policy.

Logic would dictate that constantly handing out aid (money) to persons is not a compassionate thing to do. It helps people feel compassionate, but it's not true compassion. It makes the giver feel good but really does nothing to help the recipient in the long term. The only thing that gets people out of bad situations is frustration. One might imagine that there would come a time when the frustration of poverty and the elements that follow it, such as crime, should launch a person willingly out of the situation.

A better way to help communities in need is to lower the tax burdens of everyone, including the businesses in impoverished areas, and then change may come about. When citizens get to keep more of their own money, which they've earned and not simply received, they become more prideful in how that money is spent. Lower tax rates always help to bolster economies, both nationally and locally.

High taxation on the "earners" so as to hand out money and services only confines people to a life of settling for mediocrity. They will settle for what they're given and never strive to help themselves better their situation. That shouldn't be good enough for Americans. Handing out free services on the backs of other people's hard work is a liberal politician's way of perpetuating poverty so as to get votes. Not only is that not cool, it's kind of sick.

Government Assistance

Earlier I'd acknowledged that poverty is not a blanket assessment. There are varying levels of poverty. A logic based person understands that certain people, even when given the opportunity to be great, will fail miserably. Often it's because of their actions, but sometimes life throws a curveball which sinks a person to the level of needing help. I believe in a government that has the ability to temporarily step into a person's life to assist when there is no other place for that person to turn. When family resources and private help centers (religious or not) cannot help a person, then as a society we have an obligation to step in; if not for the sake of the individual in need, then for the community as a whole. However, that obligation has been steadily widening over the past couple of generations as the net is being cast further out to define the people who need help.

I can agree that the most desperate cases of human inability to survive must be aided by a government of the people and is necessary. However, conservatives would disagree that "bad choices" of the otherwise able-bodied and able-minded constitute government assistance. Put differently: being lazy or continually fouling up does not mean a person gets to qualify for government help.

Unfortunately the line between needing assistance and being lazy has blurred dramatically; so much so that the government allows for very capable people to receive handouts like food stamps, welfare, unemployment insurance and a multitude of other benefits simply because they do not make choices in their lives that are self-sustaining. However, if the benefits suddenly stopped they'd surely find a way.

The larger problem in the government assistance model is the precedent it sets for society. A person who doesn't need the assistance or who is capable of providing for them self and still holds their hand is an example of an attitude problem; one that is being fostered by elected officials clamoring to keep their jobs. Unfortunately this makes assistance in any form more easily accessible and less stigmatized to those who simply want to take advantage of a pretty broken system.

Myself, I see it all the time when I visit places of residence for my job: folks collecting some form of government assistance sitting at home drinking booze and playing video games. When the government makes assistance seem like a human right almost, you inevitably will get many people riding the system. Lowering the standards for receiving assistance doesn't make logical sense.

On the flip side, when people find themselves in truly desperate situations, having government "safety nets" is understandable on a small scale. One of the great aspects of capitalism is that it allows people to take chances and if they fail, they have a multitude of opportunities to get themselves out without government help. But if something drastic happens on top of a person who is regrouping, so to speak, then allowing for a limited amount of help is justifiable.

It should be obvious, even to the inherently stupid, that America cannot continue to lower the standards of receiving assistance because it will eventually tip the balance such that there are not enough people providing the means for the assistance. Qualification for one to receive assistance in small quantities has become far too easy. Qualifying no longer needs much of an explanation; nor does it require accountability.

People no longer have to plead their case coherently to the government; they can simply qualify on the grounds of expenses vs. income. Unemployment benefits are given out despite the lack of true accountability of an individual's word that they are indeed looking for work. A simple online questionnaire is all that is required anymore. I know this from experience. I've collected, able-bodied and all.

The ease in obtaining assistance handed out by the government is creating justification in people's minds about receivership. There's a growing notion in the public that when one works a private or public sector job, they "pay into the system," thus are deserving of the money they receive when they're not working. What they are not told is that the amount they pay into the "system" is set up in the hopes that very few people ever need it. Nobody pays "into the system" what they will receive back in the form of unemployment insurance. If they did they'd have far less of their paycheck as is. It's just a huge farce created by people who need a constituency of hapless voters.

Conservatives don't adhere to the concept that a large government, thus they cherish personal responsibility. However, when government assistance, in so many forms, is readily available and easily accessible, the country needs a large government to handle the output. The bigger tragedy is that so much government help dilutes the sense of responsibility for one's self.

Conservatives are not heartless and we understand that people may sometimes need help. But the country would be a lot better off if the standards to receive government help were tightened. We assume that people would rather see the results of their own labor paying off for them than simply being handed something for free. Getting free money does not help people develop a sense of responsibility and thus does not seem to fit into a model of a truly free and sustainable economy.

The floodgates of assistance appear to be opening ever so greatly and unfortunately the negative stigma attached to receivership is dwindling. The government even goes so far as to give recipients receiving food stamps a credit card to swipe instead of paper vouchers so as to ease the embarrassment. If one truly needs food provided via the government, it should not be in the form of chips and salsa from the grocery store. It's almost as though it's becoming the societal norm to receive benefits at some point in one's life.

Government assistance needs to be greatly reduced, as conservatives in office always seek to do. The hope would be that eventually pride would become the driving motivator to help people get out of a hole they've created and not dependence upon other people's tax dollars. Though there's a saying that "pride will kill a man,"…if he's at the end of his rope; and there is some truth to that. However, there's another old adage about teaching a man to fish being more life sustaining than just giving him the fish. It's this concept that conservatives believe is the best way to help citizens. By tightening the standards of government assistance, we help people to rely on themselves; which in turn is better for the society as a whole.

All able-bodied and minded people have the strength and competence to provide for themselves, but the elected officials, needing to feel humanitarian, have made the process too easy and the acceptance of aid, well frankly, too acceptable. It's becoming too easy to survive while being afforded the luxury of not having to strain a relaxed lifestyle. But when one helps themselves it's better for the individual and the society.

Safety nets are a good idea for those who really need them on a very temporary basis; but too often the very capable are being lumped in with the truly needy. The solution is to develop the system so that it cannot be taken advantage, as well as creating a life sustaining mindset within the bureaucracies who facilitate the programs. Allowing people to fester in poverty, promoted by leniency, is tragic. It's certainly not cool.

Government Assistance (Part Two)

Earlier I'd acknowledged that there are some circumstances in which people do indeed need help that is funded by the society as a whole. In these cases it makes sense for the government to pick up the slack, so to speak, where the private foundations and help centers can't. Usually these are people who've exhausted a lot of the goodwill of society's volunteers. This kind of government assistance is not about unemployment checks for a few weeks or food stamps. It's the help that is necessary to sustain people who make consistently bad decisions in life that render them unable to sustain their household. Most often, unfortunately, that usually involves children in the home…and that's when the issue becomes one of life and death for the innocent.

It's unfortunate that some people put themselves in positions that require constant outside help and it's especially dreadful when there are children involved. We see this with cases of single women, some single men and/or families with two degenerate parents. Often there are multiple children and no means to attain the amount of money necessary to support them with food and clothing. This usually equates to providing government assistance via welfare for the family.

Conservatives generally do not like the idea of welfare because it means that people have put themselves in a position to need other people's money to get by. As a "here and now" solution, the ends justifies the means, but it ultimately costs the taxpayers more money to rectify someone else's problem. The general liberal defense is to allow for blame to be cast elsewhere, thus justifying the transfer of wealth. The blame gets shifted to a "broken system" or "the rich." Often, however, these bad decisions are generational and welfare families transcend time. The blame though still needs to be square on the recipients in the end.

It's not helpful to cast blame on anyone or anything else in society because blame only begets more blame and animosity. It's what advances notions like class warfare. In truth, with some help, most people can usually get themselves back on their feet because we are a resilient species capable of amazing things. Liberal politicians who want to champion the blame game or continue to feed the welfare state are pretty heartless. It's no different from bad parenting really. Undisciplined children will have a harder time understanding the concepts of endurance and perseverance in life.

Bad parenting leads to bad decisions in life on the part of the children because they're often spoiled and don't understand the difference between acquisition and reward. Conservatives want to help people, but more than that they want to help them help themselves. We understand that mistakes will be made and not everyone will go through life unscathed. But to have the government be in a position to hand out other people's money so indiscriminately is not doing anyone who needs help any real long-term good.

The condition of poverty has been a political football for decades as politicians have used it to implement government programs to make themselves feel noble. No amount of money given to able-bodied people will ever change the lifestyle that is poverty. We certainly cannot suddenly stop aiding the people whose children are now dependent on the welfare money, thus for now it will continue for the really desperate cases. But perhaps the beginning is tightening up other smaller programs like unemployment insurance and food stamps which are being abused on an incredible scale.

The small programs need to employ very strict guidelines for those who will receive them. The government officials need to be able to refuse the handing out of free gifts to those who are fully capable of work. If they can, people who would otherwise take advantage of the programs will learn to adapt or they'll be "up a creek" and on their own. There is no logical reason to be handing out free money or vouchers for people to be able to buy potato chips and soda. As well, the government needs to be aggressive about dropping people from unemployment benefits after a reasonable time. Too often people are on benefits for close to a year; that's just lazy people being lazy.

Social programs are a form of goodwill and the fact that as a society we have put such programs in place is compassion. What is not compassionate, however, is to keep persons receiving benefits believing that such aid can go on forever. Getting things for free is not teaching anyone to become self-sufficient; and our society's lifeblood is the competence of the citizens. Keeping people dependent upon taxpayer money when they can be proficient on their own is not the definition of compassion; it's pandering. That type of cajoling, offering other people's money to would-be voters, is what liberal politicians do to make it seem like they're compassionate. But it doesn't help anyone in the long run, it only hurts them.

Homelessness

Poverty has levels of seriousness and degrees to which it can be defined under, as I've stated. Perhaps the first degree is laziness, advancing in the latter stages to the real cases of human destitution. There are people who, no matter how much help they receive, cannot function and be acclimated back into society as a functioning member. A majority of these cases are people who are homeless. This level of poverty garners sympathy on a large scale because of the tragic consequences of being unable to support oneself.

It's justifiable to utilize some tax money as a collective effort to help those among us who are homeless because this condition often is the result of some mental illness. Many of these people probably wouldn't accept the conditions of an agreement involving free shelter and other services thus we help out when there is a dire need. To the extent that they do come to us in need, we can offer some temporary help. Their condition, if mentally ill, is a side effect of humanity. These are not bad people, the ones who hold up signs begging for change, they simply cannot function the way most people can.

We can probably imagine the suffering of not having adequate shelter during times of inclement weather and what kind of existence it would be. In many of these extreme cases it's not laziness per se, but mental defectiveness. Often drugs and alcohol are sought out and it only makes a bad situation worse. The defect is deeper than drugs, however. Conservatives would agree with the idea of helping these people via tax money but would also argue that we must be effective in our help. An example of such effectiveness is that we offer tax exempt status to private and religious organizations that help feed and shelter the homeless on their own accord. That's pretty cool.

Is there an answer to the homeless population that finds them becoming self-sufficient? My guess is in most cases the answer is "no," but we may be successful in some particular instances. As a society we ought to do what we can to ease suffering where we can; however we need to be honest with ourselves and know we cannot cure all human ills. We can help the homeless with basics like food and shelter when the elements call for it, but to expect taxpayers to hand over their hard earned money to be spent indiscriminately is not realistic.

Money can and does help in a lot of cases to provide some basics for people who can't provide those basics for themselves. Those cases must, however, be professionally identified and then re-verified by officials interested in helping the truly needy. Otherwise, a lack of true desire to aid the problem coupled with a listless attitude toward funding will no doubt cause the assistance to be taken advantage of by those who are capable of supporting themselves. Government can be compassionate but it must be logical about the situations of the homeless. The money needs to be used wisely and the help needs to be basic and bought cheap. Though we are a compassionate people, we also understand that our help is limited in what it can and cannot fully rectify.

Chapter 13
Social Security

There is a grand misconception about the government produced savings program called Social Security. This misconception is leading people to become less reliant on themselves for what will inevitably come in the form of their "golden years." Most people have a very basic understanding of Social Security, and in truth it's a pretty basic concept. But it's the concept that I and other conservatives have an issue with. We take issue not only with the fact that Social Security is deceiving people into believing they can shed responsibility for their retirement, but, as well, it allows government ineptitude to take over a massive program that effects every working American.

I will reiterate that the program we call Social Security is a very simple concept; not that it's justifiable however. The administration of the program entails withholding a small amount of money from an earner's paycheck, about 5-6%, with the idea that the money is then given back to the earner on a monthly basis when they reach a particular age. That's simple, no? But the problem with the program was, and is, that it's doomed to fail because it's taking the direct responsibility of saving out of the hands of the earner and putting it on the government; which has no real stake in the well being of the recipient's life.

When the program was started, the country was on its heels from the Great Depression. We can imagine that those in favor of starting the program were probably less concerned with the logistics of such an endeavor and more concerned with the appearance of doing good. Nonetheless, it probably seemed like a practical, government solution in the event of another major economic depression; lest there be thousands of elderly folks who hadn't saved for old age on the streets, cold, hungry and quickly dead. Again, if a politician feels like their duty is to save people from themselves, then this type of thing makes sense. But it's no surprise that decades after the implementation of it, Americans are saving almost nothing on their own and the program is suffocating under its own weight.

Perhaps the biggest problem Social Security faces is longevity. I don't mean that in terms of the program's ability to survive politically, but rather I'm referring to the life expectancy rates of humans in America. When the program was implemented, life expectancy for adults was lower than it is present day. This is mostly due to advances in medicine which, consequently, have led to people living healthier lives. For example, far fewer people smoke cigarettes regularly today than they did in the 1940's and 50's. Thus, what was a program initially set up to assist people for maybe 5-10 years toward the end of their life has now got to support people for 15-20 years in many cases.

The other problem with Social Security is that it has created an attitude amongst the modern working public that they "deserve" a retirement at a particular age. Currently the age a contributor becomes eligible is around 65 years. If workers begin to expect that Social Security will be the determinant as to when they will retire, thus granting them the means to survive, then the program is not being utilized the way it was meant to.

The program was no doubt set up to supplement one's own retirement efforts via their savings but too often it is becoming the sole means for people in their sunset years. However, it's ultimately up to the individual to save and calculate for themselves when they will retire. Personal responsibility should rest on the worker's shoulders not on the government's efforts to appease voting groups by promising something that isn't there.

Today's politicians, both Republican and Democrat, will echo each other's sentiments in wanting to find a way to save the Social Security program. In truth, most conservatives would rather do without the program in their personal lives and be given the option to have that money up front to do with it what they see fit. When individuals have a desire to provide for themselves, due to their sense of self-preservation, they are usually the best at deciding what to do with their resources.

The Concept of Government Savings

Conservatives hold dear the concept of personal responsibility and thus do not like the idea of the government being in control of anything that we feel we can and should manage on our own. We believe in people's capability to do for themselves, like I've mentioned previous. As well, we like having our own burdens placed on us as a matter of our own resolution; not relying on government officials or politicians to accomplish things we feel we have a responsibility for.

When politicians opine about the wonders of such programs, they are simply looking for ways to commend the job they get to do by persuading people that they in fact know how to "govern" a citizenry. It only puts more responsibility in the hands of elected and appointed officials who really have no vested interest in what's best for the individual; rather what's best for the status quo. And mediocrity is not an attribute to strive for.

Perhaps some may make the case that conservatives view government too often as "big brother" from the popular futuristic novel; an all controlling, omnipresent force. The truth is we don't think that scenario will necessarily play out, but we still don't want government thinking they know better. We simply want people to ask themselves if they really want the government taking care of things like savings and healthcare for us when we are perfectly capable of taking care for ourselves. We don't want the door to open for government officials to intrude any further despite their rhetoric about the greater good. The greater good starts with the individual. The more we let people in power do for us the more they'll continue to do.

Being watched over makes some people more comfortable and accepting of their own lack of motivation and accountability. So it makes sense that government savings plans will appeal to a particular mass of people. But conservatives know, as a responsible people, we don't need the government to save money for every person to receive later in life. It only allows less responsible people another excuse to ease one of life's basic burdens. Some on the left might call this "progressive," but it's not. Freedom is progress. Dictatorial governors and a desire for control has been the norm for most of the human civilized existence.

Logical people in government can probably agree that a program like Social Security can work similar to the previously discussed social programs such as welfare. Allowing the government to utilize some money for desperate cases of persons in their elderly existence would be right and humane. But there is no logical reason for the government to set up a savings program for able-minded people who can save for themselves. That's a freedom and a choice that individuals must make for themselves despite the modern industrial world pining for every penny to be spent on new televisions and cars.

By simply not offering a program like Social Security, government will, by default, be enhancing a society and the economy via choices made within a free market. It's akin to parents teaching children to be responsible for themselves by not making promises that appeal to the indifference and procrastination of youth. So perhaps we don't fear "big brother" but rather "big papa?"

The Third Rail

Social Security is often called the "third rail" of politics as a reference to the propelling mechanism on subway trains which is located on the tracks. The reference is actually meant to be a negative association to the discussion of reforming or "touching" the Social Security program; lest you get shocked and die! That's stupid really. Nonetheless, the narrative in political inner circles and with the liberal media is to tread lightly when talking about Social Security.

The characterization of untouchable must reside in the knowledge that the program has many recipients now who have come to rely on it. Thus to talk about reform is a dangerous political calculation for electability. But it shouldn't be and perhaps the calculation should start with the youth who haven't yet latched on to the false promises of the liberal politicians.

The reason it should be discussed as a current political topic of major reform is because the program is extremely underfunded and misused. This problem of financing needs to be addressed before the train itself derails and the promise of compensation goes up in smoke. Moving past the conservative perspective that the program is unneeded as a blanket system… how might a logical governing official fix the funding problem?

The funding problem starts with the fact that Social Security does not collect enough money from the average person to sustain 15-20 years of life; the part when care needs can add up. Nonetheless, the concept is easy, as I mentioned: take out money, save it, pay it out later. And though it is perhaps not a reasonable sum to finance every aspect of life, the money should be there. But it's not because once money is taken in to the government doles, it becomes fair game.

The irony is that government has told the American public, by means of continuing the Social Security program, that they can save money for the earner in the event the earner won't. In other words it's the government's lack of trust in the individual that propels the preservation of such programs. But the truth is the officials who are supposed to be the responsible ones have borrowed against that money, borrowed from that money and now need to borrow money to pay the recipients. This is on top of the fact that the amount of money needed to pay out is being stretched past a mere 5-10 years of life to reach well into the age of 80 plus. The math doesn't add up when it's broken down, but they're still afraid to touch it.

If we scrutinize the program's numbers problems we can see that a worker who works for 30 years will not contribute enough to fully support themselves for another 20. Both employer and worker are charged a small percentage, about 5-6% per paycheck, to be applied to the program. Adding it up to 10-12% per paycheck means that one can expect a smaller weekly or bi-weekly sum than they were used to while working. Spread that out over twenty years and you can see where the issue arises. How much less per week would someone be able to survive on during a time when they may be experiencing deteriorating heath? So the program ends up paying a person more than what they ultimately paid in. Multiply that scenario by any amount and the program will have a serious funding issue…which it does. For a program that was set up to be utilized for a very short period of time relative to a person's whole life, it is being abused and misconstrued for the advantage of those who thrive on misleading assurances.

Solution: Touch the Rail

That's right…touch the rail. Grab the thing and steer the train in a different direction. Both Republican and Democratic politicians have offered a wide range of quasi solutions to the funding problem that the program faces. Conservatives, despite not necessarily believing in the concept, have nonetheless offered solutions that, under the circumstances, seem logical. Many of those solutions begin with politicians understanding that the fund is not to be used elsewhere for any other spending. As well, they've considered investing some of the fund for a higher return. Myself, I think we ought to give earners the option of Social

Security in the first place. But Liberal politicians won't go for that.

The Democrats know that the program doesn't and can't pay for itself as is anymore, but they want the citizens to believe that it's just a technicality that can be fixed by simply taxing more from the high income earners. There are far fewer "responsible" people saving for retirement than there are not so the "soak the rich" argument plays awfully well to those who haven't bothered to save. But the program should pay for itself; it's our money after all.

The concept, however, is not reality. The age stipulations are in need of change because people are living longer and more earning is needed to pay for the program for people into their 80's and 90's. Very few people pay, as a percentage of their paycheck, enough money for the program to be a reality in today's world. Many recipients get a lot more money from the program than they'll ever pay in; because the rich are cool with paying more in than they'll ever see back.

Choice is a solution that I think would work very well if from a particular point forward lawmakers could agree to continue the program as is but give people an option to participate. In order for the "choice" principle to work, however, we will have to work to change the culture of thinking about Social Security. It must start with the younger generation who haven't yet contributed to, or have contributed very little to, the program. Perhaps we begin to offer them a choice as to whether or not they want the government to save money for them. For those of a particular age or contribution level, we can offer them lump sums or to continue on in the program. Giving people a choice on this matter would certainly force the program to become more sufficient and accountable for the money it takes in.

For the contributors who will stay in the program, it's not inconceivable that the government could raise the age of eligibility to 70. With persons living longer it's not unthinkable that some can work until the age of 70 or 75. It doesn't mean that every worker now retires at 70, but if they rely on the government to save for them, it might mean they'll have to accept some changes to a program that is antiquated in its current state. A later eligibility age would add years of earning to the program and help it become more reliable on the wages it collects alone. For those persons who save and plan, retirement may come much sooner; creating a reward factor for retiree's and getting rid of the requisite that someone or something else must save for them.

There's another solution that gets mentioned often and already happens to a degree; it's called means testing. It's really pretty unjust but it jives with the class warfare rhetoric so the left generally eats it up. For those unaware, it's a technique by which a retiring person's worth is measured at the time of retirement so as to consider withholding Social Security benefits if they're deemed too wealthy and thus don't "need" it. Of course it's easy to see where a conservative, based in logic and fairness, would have a problem with denying someone money that they've paid in.

Just because someone may be wealthy when they retire by no means qualifies their whole life. Perhaps they became wealthy toward the end of their career and were planning on using that money for family.

It's really inexplicable to try to comprehend a government that is supposed to be the governing body of "all" of the people when they constantly look for ways to extract from successful people. But to take money under the assumption a percentage of it will be returned and then not return it based upon the person's success is not ethical. It's not cool really either. If this kind of thing were done at any level of commerce there would be justifiable lawsuits and perhaps even jail time for the thieving party. It's akin to a Wall Street ponzi-scheme. This is a dangerous precedent to set, being perpetrated by people who are supposed to serve all citizens equally.

The conclusion that I and a lot of other logical thinking people will come to regarding Social Security is that should not be necessary. Government can recognize some human pitfalls and attempt to aid them but it should not need to blanket every wage earner with a tax they may or may not ever benefit from. From the initial concept of government saving for us, the program has continued to worsen over time to the extent that it is slowly reaching a point of insolvency. The concept is perhaps noble in the eyes of some politicians, but a citizenry of mostly responsible people would not need the government to save for them. Government establishes and maintains societal structure via modest regulation but it was never meant to be a body which the people rely on for their livelihood.

So we ask…can the government really begin to phase out Social Security? The answer, in short, is yes; with the right people and a changing of attitude. It's certainly not impossible to begin to change the attitudes of government reliance, especially among the young. Discontinuing the program would perhaps scare some people, and as humans we can all understand the feelings of uncertainty. The allure of the program is that it provides people with a way to shed the responsibility of retirement savings in an increasingly fast-paced world. Admittedly at times taking care of "today" seems hard enough, but just because something is hard doesn't mean it requires a government solution.

The backbone of conservative thought is a motivation to do for oneself and to help others to realize their potential to do for themselves. Allowing people to take chances and learn to be self-sufficient is real freedom. When people anchor savings and other self-reliant means to the government ship they are going to sail the way other people want to go instead of steering the boat themselves. The outcome of relying on oneself is far more rewarding than not. It's far cooler too; relying on oneself. Savings, as with most things in life, are more gratifying when achieved individually through hard work and personal endeavor. Perhaps the exception to that is sex, which is usually best when carried out in a shared effort. Note, I did say usually…some people, ya know?

Chapter 14
Immigration

The issue of immigration has, and will continue to, ebb and flow as a hot button issue on the political playing field. When liberal politicians feel as though immigration heart-strings need to be tugged, in an effort to get votes, they like to bring it up in an attempt to pin conservatives into a corner. It's not really an issue to be solved politically as much as it is a problem that needs to be upheld lawfully. The laws on the books about immigration to this country are set, logical and do not need bending or to be set aside for certain groups of people. But when the left needs an issue, they use immigration in an attempt to make conservatives look like they don't like immigrants in general; especially the ones with brown skin. In a perfect world, that kind of race-baiting would be met with a swift slap to the face…in an effort, not to maim, but knock sense into the accusers.

Conservatives take a different approach to "solving" the immigration issue than do liberals because we often think the way of life in America is superior to that of any other place on Earth. Liberals don't like that kind of "superior" talk. Conservatives love for country also translates to the desire to protect this way of life from potential lawlessness and disorder. The reason immigration is a political and legal issue is because there are millions of people who've come to this country illegally; skirting the system set up to protect American citizens.

When people enter the country illegally-when there are clearly stated procedures, not to mention thousands of others waiting to get their chance legally-it relays a negative message to the current citizens. Too often liberals want to grant legal status based on longevity. But their argument is transparent because their real motivation is in building on a constituency which relies on government to ease the burdens of the world for them.

To address the misconception liberals throw out to the media and whoever else will listen: conservatives do not hate immigrants, illegal or otherwise. What we don't like is the notion that some illegal immigrants feel like they can hide behind liberalism in an effort to show that legal immigration laws should not pertain to them. If that's the case, it's a bad message indeed to send to a country which prides itself in its ability to have freedom and lawfulness coexist in relative harmony; unlike the dictatorships and oppressive regimes in many other places on Earth. Trust me when I say conservatives understand the plights of immigrants who want to flee terrible regimes around the world. But pinning the costs and responsibility on Americans by way of illegal immigration is not the way to ultimately go about it. No matter what the situation, the immigrating party must show responsibility and respect for the law on their part.

It Starts At Home

Immigration to this country is often done by persons from countries or territories that are not as grand as the United States in terms of living conditions and economic opportunities. Thus, they come here to better their lives; which makes conservatives proud. It says a lot about the place we live and work every day to maintain and improve. That furthers the idea that we want to protect it from nefarious persons who may attempt to immigrate illegally and subsequently turn to crime. But not only do we want to protect it from bad people who may slip over, we also understand that many of the laws were created in an attempt to grow at a sustainable pace and not inundate the economy with too many workers and not enough opportunity.

An economy will grow in time to fit a population that grows with it. If we allow too many people to enter the economy at any given time, the opportunities initially will become scarcer; especially for the current citizens whose wages may suffer as a result. The economy should be left to grow relative to the available workforce with a reasonable amount of able-bodied workers allowed to enter it. Even if the opportunities appear to be there, too much manipulation is not a good thing for the market.

Those are just some of our reasons for wanting to control immigration and they should be respected by persons who want to come here. Applying for and going through a procedure to attain American citizenship is something that should be a badge of honor and not a free ride on the taxpayer dole; handed out with eventual reluctance. America has rules for a reason. Liberals politician's desire for creating unnecessary regulations is apparent in many facets of life, but following a few logical procedures to citizenship is not unpractical. The procedure is no doubt somewhat muddled in red tape, but that's not a good excuse to circumvent the process.

Conservatives understand the desires on the part of family members to reunite when some have immigrated legally and are waiting for other family to come. And for people living in countries or societies that are not well-governed and have little opportunity available for its citizens, we feel for them too. Perhaps some American citizens take for granted what they have in terms of real freedom and opportunity. As for myself, I couldn't imagine living anyplace else. That being the case, we still have to approach immigration with a sense of responsibility for the sake of the current citizens of America. The government must enact better authority and control over the problem that is illegal immigration. It cannot be used as a political pawn simply because it's an issue that deals with human relations.

Cheap Labor

Despite the fact that it is ultimately the responsibility of the immigrating individual to do so legally, there is another culprit in the game that fuels the temptation of illegal immigration. This culprit, who is the person or company that hires illegal workers, enables people who have immigrated illegally by offering jobs to them and helping them avoid detection and continue to stay for work. The allure is high, no doubt, for companies and business owners to hire labor at a price much lower than would be demanded by a legal worker. This is especially true in low-skilled labor; fields that can generally take on many illegal workers. It's understandable because it lowers overhead costs and offers work to people who are willing to do it for less; picking cherries ought not be a $10.00/hr job. Hiring cheap labor becomes more attractive considering the high cost of business regulation slapped on by government.

The result is negative two-fold: first, it takes positions away from legal workers despite the inflated minimum wage standards; second, it ultimately puts the illegal worker in a precarious position should he or she get caught and get deported after uprooting from their native home. It gives people false hope that they will be able to stay when the system is not set up for them to enter the country this way.

Unfortunately, illegal immigrants often obtain false identification that, even when easily recognized as fake, will get accepted by the hiring party. On many levels this kind of hiring can be potentially hazardous. Liability alone should dictate that these hiring practices are not wise. In a litigation hungry society, any accidents that befall a worker or bystander would no doubt be means for a hefty lawsuit. Not to mention the costs incurred by the taxpayers if there are medical damages that cannot be paid for.

The easy solution is to put heavy penalties on business owners who hire illegal immigrants without having gone through the federal system set up to check a person's status. In other words, hiring those who don't have proper and verified identification should be met with hefty fines. There are systems in place that can be utilized by employers to ensure they're hiring someone with legal status. In a competitive market place, it gives employers an unfair advantage if they are hiring illegal workers for less of a wage. As well, abetting the false hope of illegal workers that they'll be protected by their employer is not commendable. It is a risk taken by the illegal worker, no doubt, but the employer is the one who knows better what the consequences can be.

The ultimate goal would be an economy in which illegal workers are not needed, and thus not sought out. We can achieve this by relaxing minimum wage standards for low-skilled labor, easing unnecessary regulations put on businesses and lowering tax burdens for businesses and individuals. It's hard to blame the employer for the desire to take a chance on getting an edge, but doing so has caused a bigger problem than could have been anticipated. The lawbreakers, on both sides, are hoping to appease the politicians by playing the sentimental fools. But we shouldn't reward lawless behavior regardless of what's attached to it. That…is not cool.

Taking Ownership

Perhaps the best reason to encourage and enforce legal immigration is to ensure that the immigrating party invests themselves in their move; thus giving them some skin-in-the-game via taxes, voting and other responsibilities that come with citizenship. When a person wants to immigrate to the United States legally, they must make major preparations to secure legal residency, a job, a place to live and most importantly, understand the decision is something they feel is best for them. However, if they simply slip across the border or visit and don't leave, by their actions, they're not displaying the kind of ethics and morals we would want from a new citizen.

When persons do not take the time or effort to immigrate legally to America the message they're sending is undoubtedly one of disregard and defiance toward the structure of this country. The fact that it's relatively simple to enter this country illegally and avoid detection leads to the inevitable possibility that some immigrants will eventually turn to a life of crime. Don't misread or misinterpret that last sentence, because it's not a blanket statement. However, if a person is in the country illegally and finds themself unable to get work, turning to crime might be an easy avenue considering the likely scenario, if convicted, would be deportation instead of a lengthy incarceration.

It's true that many people who emigrate or want to emigrate from other areas of the world to America probably don't have many resources, making the process even more difficult. Thus, illegal immigration is often an easier route. Most who come want only to make a better life for themselves, and that is commendable. But if it's really worth it to them to make a change for the better, they ought to seek to do it legally. The United States is by no means the only country in the world with immigration standards and admittance procedures, but perhaps it's one of the worst at enforcement.

The electorate in every state should encourage politicians to make immigration something that is an investment for potential citizens. When a person takes ownership of the process to becoming a citizen of the United States, it's better for everyone. As well, harsh punishment needs to be the penalty for breaking the rules of legal immigration. What that amounts to is deportation for the offending party, regardless of their circumstances. It's severe but it should be remembered that it's ultimately a burden that's put on the immigrating party to do so legally. It shouldn't be a source of blame or guilt for current citizens to who want to uphold the laws.

Green (Race) Card

Immigration is a fiery topic in politics primarily because liberal politicians, and some diehard constituents, love to make it into more of an issue about race than actual law and procedure. Race is often used in the immigration argument because liberals really have very little merit to their political stance on this. As previously stated, liberal politicians want to grant amnesty to a group of people they know will return the favor in the way of votes.

Playing the race card in this circumstance is unfortunate because the issue is not about race. Liberals are well aware that the majority of illegal and legal immigration is done by persons from Mexico and Central and South America, so they pretend that conservative's objection to amnesty for illegal persons must be based on race. Of course, they're as empty as their rhetoric.

Conservatives realize that America is one of the only places on Earth in which you can succeed based upon your ability and not on your race. Capitalism and the free market system doesn't discriminate because it deals in dollars and if you have a great idea or great work ethic you'll succeed no matter where your starting point is.

Many of the countries in which folks emigrate from do not allow citizens to truly stretch the boundaries of their abilities. These places are either in constant governmental turmoil or wallowing in the ineptitude of a broken government. Conservatives love to hear stories of people coming from the ashes of nothing and becoming successful because we understand that's why this country is so grand; the opportunity it gives everyone.

It's logical to conclude that people who make the effort to come to the United States legally will have the best chance to succeed because they won't be living under a blanket of anonymity. It could be argued that legal immigration generally yields the hardest workers, the most eager to succeed and a population that truly wants to become American. It's what would bring out the best in our immigrating population. It would probably bring out the coolest as well.

The United States can be a saving grace for some and a bold opportunity for others, but it needs people that want to come here for the right reasons; as well as lawfully. Some illegal immigrants may have great intentions and aspirations, but their immigration has the potential to end very negatively. It's certainly not a race issue, it's a logic issue. Wanting the best for one's country via lawful behavior is not racist.

People and politicians that turn immigration into a race issue by implying there may be a racial component to conservative values as it pertains to legal immigration are truly clueless. Perhaps it is they who are generally uncomfortable with the notion that different races are coming together with a common goal of freedom. They'd no doubt prefer immigrants come here to be taken care of by the state. Maybe it's a reflection of their own beliefs, thus they point the finger elsewhere so as to not be revealed.

Wanting to live by guidelines and rules is not racist. Expecting others to respect those rules is also not racist, however much one agrees or disagrees with the particular rules. America has a good reason for wanting immigration to happen at a pace that doesn't suffocate our economy nor break the rules of law. There are good reasons, as well, to ensure that immigrants are properly vetted and the country is not harboring escaped criminals from other countries. America has a system set up to allow for people to immigrate to this country and it should be followed and respected. When it's not, it is hard to attach positive feelings. It's not a race issue.

America is proof that many different people from many different backgrounds can work effectively together and individually to better their lives. It may be appropriate to tell liberals to "zip it" when they begin to turn immigration into a race issue. They obviously need time to get over themselves and their constant need to make themselves look noble by bringing others down. Substance appears to be severely lacking in the immigration-equals-race argument. It's an easy one to shut down if one has logic and truth on their side…combined with a good chunk of coolness.

What Now?

In concluding the issue of immigration let me address, in my opinion, what I think could be a quasi-solution to the burgeoning population of undocumented, unaccounted for, and illegally residing people in the United States. The politicians and powers that be will rack their heads with solutions of how best to appease or sound less offensive in their effort to create a solution to the illegal immigrant problem.

The elected officials are occasionally pushed to create a resolution because generations of office holders before them dragged their heels and thus it has created a problem. It would not set a good precedent for the United States to suddenly forgive the illegal status of millions of people and wipe the slate clean on their immigration status. If that's done, it will inevitably lead to the country being inundated further with more illegal people expecting the same resolution to be sought over time. Simply coming over illegally and setting roots down and expecting amnesty should not be a cycle of immigration that the country could or should perpetuate.

The logical solution is to keep consistent with the laws as they are written and deport people who are here illegally once they are caught. There are millions of people waiting to come to the country legally when their opportunity arises and illegal immigration severely hampers their prospects. Admittedly, deportation en masse is not a news story the politicians want to be seen supporting, but the blame can stretch back for generations.

Despite any political outrage or cable news hysteria that would undoubtedly follow a massive deportation effort, the blame is not on the one's upholding the law. The majority of the blame is on the offending party; the ones who broke the law by entering illegally. Perhaps it can be said the blame be shared, to an extent, with prior generations of lawmakers who have let the immigration problem balloon from a lack of enforcement, but that's not a reason to allow for amnesty.

There is an underlying problem, however, and it is one that time has helped to manifest into a "sticky" situation. Some of the illegal immigrants have surely been in the country long enough that they now have one or multiple children who have been born here. They have housing, jobs and family that have been established for some time. Approaching the problem with these variables means that logic has to consider them.

If, for example, two adults from Mexico emigrated ten years ago and have multiple children who may be in school, it's hard to look at those children and label them as not American. Unfortunately children often will be affected by their parent's actions, whether negative or positive. It wouldn't be impossible to say that the whole family needs to be deported, but it's certainly a tough position to put the American citizens in.

If we look at it through the prism of the family it makes the situation one that nobody wants to deal with harshly. But the country cannot begin to allow people to make the choice to break the law and be forgiven because they've had children; otherwise that may open the conversation up to other breakers of law who get caught years later. For example: a person robs a bank but does not get caught for five years. When they're apprehended, they have a new born baby. Does he or she get to avoid the penalty of robbery based on the fact that they have a child and would be missed at home? No they don't because that's not logical. One can weigh the crimes differently but nonetheless, family matters cannot trump basic law.

On a transitory basis, the government could enact a temporary stay that allows persons with families, who are apprehended for illegal status, time to make the deportation process work. The adults will get time to register and continue to work but the government sets a deportation date and the adults must adhere to that. They can be granted legal status until that time, but they cannot attain citizenship simply by "waiting it out."

In particular instances, however, some illegal immigrants need to be granted the opportunity to stay indefinitely with "legal status," due to circumstances which make them undoubtedly American. Government officials can set guidelines for those circumstances. Of course, any legislation which allows for legal status to be granted must be coupled with ironclad border protection.

Regardless of how relaxed the enforcement has been on the part of American lawmakers and authority, we can't avoid the fact that the process began with an infraction; of which the penalty is ultimately deportation. Illegal immigrants cost the American taxpayers a lot of money and jobs. It may seem unfair but matters such as these ones need to be dealt with, void of emotion, or it will simply snowball to the extent that taxpayers cannot afford.

Chapter 15
Foreign Policy

How countries interact with each other has, for generations, helped ultimately to define what real freedom is and to what measures people will go to defend it. As a political topic, foreign policy doesn't garner the attention like many domestic issues do because to most Americans it seems…well…foreign. It usually entails a summit or meeting or speech to the leaders of other nations; usually filled with rhetoric that deals in billions of dollars. It's tuned out, most likely, because issues that confront us on the shores of our own land seem to be of a more valued urgency. The policies our government adheres to when dealing with other countries are important, not only because we want to protect our way of life, but we also want other nations to understand the opportunities and grandeur of a free society.

Perhaps the apathetic attitude towards foreign policy and why it generally only appears to grab attention during times of conflict is because it may be hard to measure how our government should react and handle other governments. As the world shrinks, in terms of people's ability to travel and communicate globally, the less we may consider the globe to be "foreign." Though the reality is there are still some very dangerous places on Earth which would certainly not be suitable for a family vacation without dad packing a separate suitcase full of firearms. Nonetheless, America's interactions with other governments should reflect the values and principles in which the country was fought for.

Conservatives approach foreign policy no different than they do domestic policy. That's to say that logic still needs to triumph despite the fact that not every country's governing personnel shares our same admiration for freedom. America's government cannot abandon its sense of pragmatism simply because leadership in other countries doesn't structure their societies in such a way that it helps its citizens prosper and enjoy real freedom. In other words we need to be cool when dealing with regimes which have severe stability issues.

Unfortunately America does get involved in the composition of other nations, often when it should probably leave well enough alone. Often that involvement is through the gifting of money or resources. One can understand the logic behind such charity if it's done with the intention of spreading the benefits of freedom and capitalism. The more people who benefit from the prosperities of freedom, the more it protects us from threats that loom from misguided ideologies and rogue religious interpretations. Thus, if America can help, it ought to. But logic dictates that there is only so much good that giving taxpayer money can do. If the charitable efforts are not met with measurable improvement toward that goal, then the money should cease to be given.

Without firsthand knowledge of "closed door" meetings between leaders of the world, I can only assess based on what I read or see covered by news organizations. What I gather is that the biggest contribution we make to other nations around the world is money. Perhaps the money would be better spent if it were in the form of "how to" guides to becoming more like America, nevertheless our government does give exorbitant amounts of taxpayer money to other nations. Some might argue it buys goodwill, and to an extent it may. As well, it may help to cultivate natural resources the United States ultimately benefits from via trade relations. But logical people must ask: does giving money really solve any long term problems? It's no different than domestic government give-aways; it doesn't move a person (or country) up it only keeps them where they are.

The United States government should operate very carefully when it comes to the "who" and "what" taxpayer money supports. If the money is being used to support terrorism or warfare amongst rival factions, then the money is being misused. If the taxpayers of America are going to hand over their hard earned money, there's no debate that the money should be accounted for and used in a way that helps citizens of the receiving country. Whether that's through direct aid or with infrastructure that advances the probabilities of self-reliance, it must be used honorably and honestly.

The endgame should be self-sufficiency and freedom manifesting in the countries we aid with taxpayer money. Why would Americans expect anything less with the money that they earn being given to dictatorial regimes? If the money is not accounted for and there are no signs of progress toward self-reliance, the money should be withheld. It is not unreasonable to have expectations of the receiving countries that they work to become less dependent on foreign aid; America's or any other nation's charity. As a gesture of humanity, America should help out where there is human suffering, to the extent it can, but even that aid should come with some stipulations. Simply handing out taxpayer money cannot be mistaken for foreign policy, regardless of the intentions or where it may rank on the bleeding-heart scale of coolness.

War

There is a purposely misguided narrative in the American ideological debate from persons on the left that conservatives generally want to settle foreign disputes with war; flexing the country's military muscles. Though conservatives would like to see the world embrace freedom, there is no precedent for the desire to engage in war as a tactic to solve problems. War is hell, or so I'm told, and no person in good conscience could send military personnel to a dangerous environment without clear and logical motivations and clearly defined objectives. Conservatives embrace military action in terms of self defense and sometimes that self defense involves allies of the country. America does and should ally itself with countries that share similar beliefs in governance and human rights, and if any of the allies are attacked then as a group there should be action taken.

War and foreign policy could be thought of in terms of a neighborhood setting, to simplify it. In most neighborhoods there are many houses in relative close proximity. Most households are probably familiar with the people who occupy the houses directly around their own and in some cases probably have friends who live down the street or around the corner. Not all houses will be "neighborly" with each other, but no doubt there are acquaintances and familiar faces. This analogy of a neighborhood could be applied to the world and the various countries. Some border each other and some are "down the street (across the globe)." Within that neighborhood there are good neighbors and bad neighbors; it's the actions of the bad neighbors which determines how the good neighbors must handle them.

Foreign policy need not be terribly complex, in theory. Within the neighborhood, neighbors generally look out for one another. If one neighbor begins to act like a jerk toward another, unprovoked, then the other neighbors might step in to help. America has neighbors and friends and it will come to the defense of those friends if one of their neighbors starts a fight. If the fight happens to be between two bad neighbors, the neighborhood should keep an eye on it so it doesn't spill out into the streets and become a neighborhood brawl. The United States is good and it has great friends and neighbors who will all help out in crisis.

Conservatives view on war and military use is simple logic: if the use of force is necessary to defend the country or help out a neighbor, then the ability to do so should be utilized. It's near impossible to use dialogue alone to convince the bad neighbors to stop their bad actions. Sometimes it's necessary to use force when the bad neighbors act out. War means people, fathers, brothers, mothers and sisters die; it's a policy that must be taken seriously. Conservatives value life, sacrifice, and our way of life. We value the things we have been blessed with in life and if someone tries to take them from us then it's necessary to fight back.

Understanding that the United States has been involved in some otherwise not so successful military actions only means that we should continue to learn from the past. Going into conflict too quickly or without a well planned military strategy seems pretty foolish. No person should think that war is a values game; it's not. The military of the United States is the best there's ever been. To abuse it would be foolish. To use it when not definitively necessary would be criminal. War is never an answer but it can be a hard remedy for a difficult situation.

Hindsight

The United States has no doubt had some foreign and domestic policies in its past that were not quite up to modern day standards. Many on the left will gleefully point out America's flawed past as a way to avoid generational guilt they may be feeling. However, when people use a stain in history to paint with a broad brush it's done to incite negative feelings. Whether it is colonialism or slavery, the left loves to use these policies as a way to demonize America as a whole. For some reason they feel the burdens of the past generation's mistakes are theirs to correct and they feel like speaking against America as a whole makes them noble and above reproach. It's OK to discuss policies of the past but not to condemn the people of that era based upon today's evolved standards.

Discourse that places blame in an effort to shield oneself is listless and transparent. Yet many on the left, including very decorated persons in education, will continue to assault previous generations based on standards that today's society holds. It's done to gather momentum for someone else's animosity. If there are people who want to rail against the past, so be it. America is but one country with some black marks in history. But it's important to keep in mind that people in the past did not have the same understanding that today's society does when it comes to many facets of life. The world was a very big place then and for whatever reason it was viewed very differently. Even very religious people, who believed in the uniqueness of human life, made mistakes about the value of the lives of others. Allowing animosity over such historical matters, however, is pointless; with the exception of inciting anger.

People who will further the notion that America's failings are in need of retribution of some fashion are typical. They use very emotional reasoning to stir up negative feelings; and unfortunately it is usually done by means of race and gender. In other words, the white American male is the root of all evil. Of course that line of thinking is often regurgitated by those who lack the motivation to overcome hardship and strife. Blame is a much easier emotion than optimism. If the lack of understanding gave us injustices of the past, then continuing to perpetuate negative feelings of such will not advance us any further. Nobody should get too hung up on the past when the future can always be changed. And purpose driven change, when logical, is very cool indeed.

Chapter 16
The End

I'm not one who generally enjoys long goodbyes so I won't make this chapter one of them. Whether it's the end of a long stay with relatives or simply the end of a song, I'm of the opinion that the "goodbye" be wrapped up quickly in an effort to avoid the perception that one is never coming back. Thus, in keeping with that philosophy, relative to the rest of the book this chapter will be brief. However I must, as all good authors do, consolidate and reiterate my point in an effort to get the reader to "tie it all together…" one last time. I'm not really a good author, but I hear the good ones do that!

The most important thing to remember when it comes to politics is that the biggest difference between conservative and liberal ideology is the concept of individualism; which determines how much government is perceived to be needed. Conservatives embrace individualism, which means they do not see a need for an ever expanding government influence.

Individualism generally subscribes to the notion that having and effective, but limited, government is the best way to govern the natural yearning for freedom that humans possess. Using the government as a nurturer of the people is generally thought to be a recipe for the slow deterioration of that freedom.

If human beings had the gift of fulltime dignity, charm and grace and were able to maintain well behaved relationships, we could make the case that little to no government would be needed. What oversight would a citizenry of angels really need? But the reality is, as humans, we have flaws that require objective governmental structure. The good news is that for the most part we're able to understand the reasons and thus play by the rules. But sometimes the rules are not made with objectivity and as a result, we need logical people to obtain bureaucratic and political positions. That's why voting matters.

The mechanism that gives our government its strength is the previously mentioned agreement between the governed and the governors, but as well its ability to be operated by regular people. However, as the governed we often allow nonsensical resolutions by way of apathy and subsequently we relinquish particular freedoms almost unknowingly. The success of the United States has been due to the limited powers of the government. Indeed the country is a fabulous success story in relation to human history and it's despite government, not because of it.

A community of people is not inherently helpless structurally; rather they are enhanced by a moderate sense of organization and framework communally. Some oversight on humanity is needed but the majority of solutions do not need to be government-produced. The conscious limiting of government is what works to thwart calculated hierarchy and oppression. People need to be free from government intrusion even when such encroachment is done under the veil of protection. In other words…we don't always need a soft landing because it's the impact, not the fall, which people learn the greatest lesson from.

My hope is that by writing this book about "why" conservatives take the positions we do, some perspectives can change. Unfortunately many people are led to believe that the conservative ideology is the more restrictive of the philosophies. Conservatives are not reactionary in nature but as well we're not knee-jerk. Solutions need to be logical and government needs to be objective. The logistics of government and its functions will change over time, but it's the purpose or the "spirit" of governing that should remain static. Government is a referee, not an influence.

Points to Remember

Many apolitical people are consistently targeted by those on the left to conclude that Republicans and conservatives are a hindrance to progress. They do this because they either need votes or they need to shed feelings of guilt. But remember…

- DON'T PUT TOO MUCH FAITH IN ELECTED OFFICIALS

    They do not know any better simply because they

hold elected office. We need people elected who value individualism and understand logic and objectivity. We do not need consistent infiltration into society in an effort to shape it into conformity. Government is best when necessary, functional and, most importantly, limited. Government is not the holder of rights for citizens, it's the protector. Humans have rights because they're alive; government simply ensures those rights are upheld.

- PEOPLE HAVE THE ABILITY TO BE GREAT AND THE LUXURY OF BEING MEDIOCRE

It's important to remember, however, that one man's mediocre is another's great. People are different from one another and they will always be. Thus we thrive when society is structured and governed in a way that allows for those differences to manifest into their own versions of success. If government or bureaucrats attempt to move some citizens to societal levels which do not match their own efforts it inevitably restrains the yearning to do for one's self. No other place on Earth has ever given humans the capacity to succeed the way the United States has.

- GOVERNMENT DOES NOT HAVE MONEY, CITIZENS DO

We give it to the government in an agreement that it will carry out certain duties. Everything the government does or spends our money on *can be changed*. The government is not an "all-knowing" entity but rather just people. People don't always have the same ideas, but it starts with understanding the intention of government and reacting accordingly. Citizens can choose how they want to be governed and they should take that seriously. People that want to use government to further agendas and govern with limited or no objectivity should be recognized and, of course, not voted for.

- THINK LOGICALLY...FOR GOVERNMENT'S SAKE

Logic is a very simple concept. Whether the issue is abortion or taxes, logic should dictate the choices made. We should not let government get away with creating illogical solutions or creating solutions to problems which do not exist. America was founded on the principle of limited government and that is a pretty damn cool concept.

- VOTE RIGHT

I wasn't born into riches and I've never been a member of a country club. My beliefs about conservatism, in other words, are not instilled due to a feeling of obligation based on a wealthy lineage. I say that because many liberals think conservative persons are all wealthy and greedy (or hillbillies). I'm not a hillbilly either! I'm not conservative because I'm a Republican; instead it's the exact opposite. It didn't take me long, once I paid close enough attention, to figure out what made sense.

It's my belief that conservative elected officials have the best in mind for all Americans and not just for the ones they feel they can siphon votes from. Conservative Republicans are, by virtue of their own virtues, the party of the "little guy." They want America to succeed and they understand that government cannot will that to happen. Voting for conservative Republicans will allow America to grow and prosper while government begins to recede. And that, by any measure, has got to be cool.